WA

1915–1919

With best wishes
from
Graham

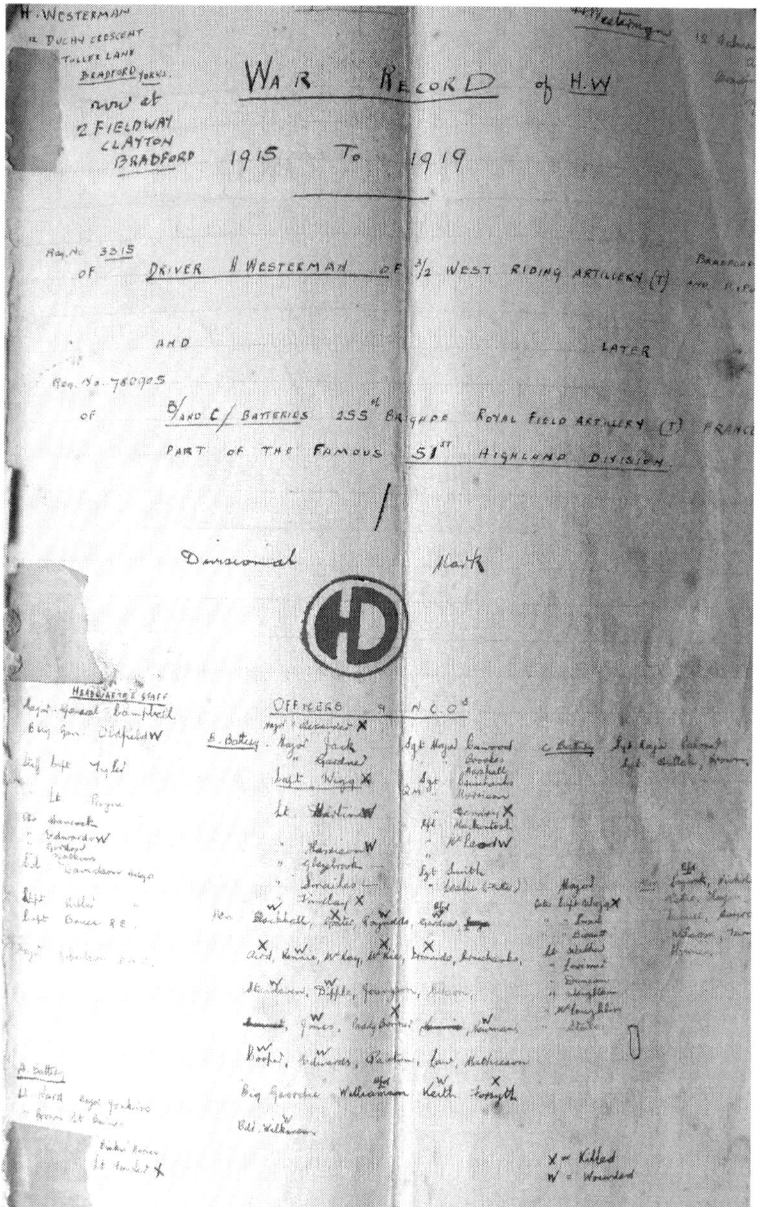

H. WESTERMAN
12 DUCHY CRESCENT
TOLLER LANE
BRADFORD YORKS.
now at
2 FIELDWAY
CLAYTON
BRADFORD

WAR RECORD of H.W

1915 TO 1919

Reg. No 3315
OF DRIVER H WESTERMAN OF 3/2 WEST RIDING ARTILLERY (T)

AND LATER

Reg. No. 780905
OF B/ AND C/ BATTERIES 255th BRIGADE ROYAL FIELD ARTILLERY (T) FRANCE
PART OF THE FAMOUS 51ST HIGHLAND DIVISION

Divisional Mark

HEADQUARTER'S STAFF
Major General Campbell
Brig Gen. Oldfield W

OFFICERS & N.C.O.s

B. Battery. Major Jack
Sgt Major
Capt Wigg X
Lt.
Sgt Smith

C Battery

A. Battery
Major Jenkins

Big Geordie Williamson Keith Forsyth

X = Killed
W = Wounded

abt 60 Horses Killed at A Batt

WAR RECORD
1915–1919

HARRY WESTERMAN

*

no. 3315 DRIVER WESTERMAN
3/2 WEST RIDING ARTILLERY

*

no. 780905 B AND C BATTERIES 255TH BRIGADE
ROYAL FIELD ARTILLERY

*

EDITED BY

GRAHAM BURGESS

2014

For Jean Burgess, neé Westerman.
My mother
and Harry's daughter

FIRST PUBLISHED 2014

ISBN 978 1 502 57221 9

Designed and typeset by
Lyn Davies Design

CONTENTS

WAR RECORD

Harry Westerman in Whitby 1951

PREFACE

HARRY WESTERMAN was my maternal grandfather, born in 1894. He died at the age of 67 when I was two years old. As my childhood progressed I began to hear rumours of a mysterious 'diary' which he had written during his time in the First World War. Indeed, it turned out to be something of a family legend, so I was somewhat awestruck when, as a teenager, I was finally allowed to see it and know that it was real. As I read it, what struck me was more the power of writing than the horrors of the war, and this has stayed with me. Of all my many ancestors Harry Westerman alone, through his surviving writing, has retained the ability to speak to me and reveal something of who he had been. The rest are silent. Yet there was also a frustration in reading his *War Record* in that there are many entries which suggest he did a great deal of additional writing which has not survived. Indeed my mother recalls her own mother discarding bundles of his letters after her husband's death. This was probably not so much due to any sensitive personal material, but rather because she did not recognise their historical value. By the early 1960s the First World War was ancient history and another war had intervened and not long been over. Commemoration of the event was waning and it was not until much later that the pivotal importance of that war on especially the British psyche, the subsequent political direction of Europe and the whole cultural history of the twentieth century began to be more generally recognised.

ABOUT THE TEXT

The diary which has survived was compiled by Harry Westerman in 1923 directly from notes he'd kept in the field. In fact soldiers were expressly forbidden to keep such accounts as it was felt that these could contain information useful to the enemy if they were to fall into the wrong hands – although there are many surviving examples. There are daily entries from his joining up in October 1915 until the end of that year. Entries for 1916 are not dated nor so extensive although they do give a picture of his movements and his various daily routines. Perhaps it was a New Year's resolution in that from January 1st 1917 until his demobilisation in 1919 there is hardly a day without an entry. His style is clipped and understated, factual rather than emotional, always starting with the weather. Yet, despite this, the diary tells a clear and extraordinary story of his time in France, unloading ships, his lucky breaks playing piano, being left behind due to illness and being put, as a Yorkshireman, into the 51st Highland Division; then to the front supplying gun batteries in the mud and chaos, interspersed with playing piano and writing letters home. He has several close calls and many of his colleagues are killed or wounded. The normalisation of an otherwise barely endurable reality becomes at times almost surreal:

> *June 4th 1917*
> Up line at 4:00 am with ammunition. Shelled with 8 inch. Forsyth killed and one wounded. Shells dropping too near to be healthy. Harness cleaning in afternoon. Playing in cricket match in evening First man in, scored 3.

It is clear from his account that Harry was almost as appalled at the number of horses killed as we was of the men. His tone also becomes steadily more critical of the wisdom of some of the orders routinely given as the war progresses.

The *War Record* builds to a terrible climax at the famous last battle of Cambrai in October 1918, followed closely by his going on leave back to the relative normality of Bradford.

> *November 7th 1918*
> Caught 8:50am from St Pancras, arrived Bradford 2:45pm. No one to meet me. Fancy.

The back cover of the handwritten *War Record* is entitled 'Remarks re-anything' and includes some analysis of the lessons learned along with a list of his horses, major battles and a later entry made during WWII.

In addition to the *War Record,* there is also a small autograph book which had been given to Harry for Christmas 1911. He evidently carried this with him throughout the war and it served him as a sketch-book, a place for occasional writing and as a place where others were invited to write or draw. Many of the entries are dated and excerpts are included at relevant points in the text.

The political and strategic course of the war is well enough known, yet the individual experiences of it are all different and remarkable. Like many men, Harry Westerman did not speak much about the war after it was over, except possibly with others who had been there and could understand; so we are privileged then, to hear him speak to us now, through this, his *War Record.*

Graham Burgess
May 2014

Harry Westerman, age 22. Front, centre.

On leave, 1918

BIOGRAPHY

HARRY WESTERMAN was born October 12th 1894 in Bradford, Yorkshire, one of seven children, with three brothers and three sisters. They lived in Otley Road, a poor area of Bradford (which has since been extensively redeveloped), in a three bedroom house with an outside toilet and no hot running water – although significantly they did have a piano. The boys shared a bed in one room, the girls in another and their parents in the third. The family was firmly working-class and remained very close. Harry went to Wapping School nearby which, although in a deprived area, nonetheless had a good headmaster and a good reputation. He also attended a nearby church where he sang in the choir and was able to play the organ. It is said that his future wife had gone to hear him sing there as he was reputed to have had a lovely voice, and that this is how they had first met.

After secondary school Harry went to the mechanics' Institute (the forerunner of the technical college), although he was not, by all accounts, a very practical man. He started work as a wool-sorter, grading wool into different qualities at a mill, and this is what he was doing when he was called up in 1915.

During the war one brother, Wilfred, died (burst appendix) and another, Tom, the eldest, was wounded in France and for the rest of his life had to wear a large built-up boot on one foot.

After the war, Harry was once again employed as a wool-sorter. In 1925 he married Winifred Elsie Crowther. She was the daughter of Charles Crowther, the owner of a small woollen mill who gave Harry a job as a sales rep. Later in the 1920s, possibly as a result of the financial crisis, the company failed and Harry was made redundant. He, and his new wife, were at this time renting a house in Pasture Lane, Clayton (Bradford). However, following the death of her husband,

Winifred's mother bought a house in Fieldway, Clayton, which they shared with her, to be joined in 1930 by their only child, Jean, my mother. As well as some part-time work for the Halifax Building Society, Harry eventually became a self-employed agent for 'Gabardine', an occupation in which he did not particularly thrive. It is also evident that class tensions were an enduring feature of family life.

It is abundantly clear to me that Harry was essentially a musician, albeit one who had to endure uninspiring work in order to make ends meet (and I recognise a certain atavistic inheritance in this respect). Music was his passion and it served him well throughout his life in spite of all the dangers and difficulties he faced. He had offered to teach music theory to servicemen in France in 1919, was organist at Clayton Methodist Church for many years (having missed getting the same post at the Anglican Church due to his late return from France). He ran his own choir and during the Second World War conducted the Clayton Brass Band.

HARRY WESTERMAN'S WAR

Harry Westerman joined up as a 'driver', that is, a horse-driver for the Royal Field Artillery. He had no great experience of horsemanship before this, however, it was his musical abilities which serve him particularly well and he found himself frequently playing piano at officers' messes, various musical and dramatic productions and later at dances and cinemas - and regularly getting paid for it. Indeed, it is interesting in itself to note just how much entertainment was available to the soldiers not far from the more familiar mud and trenches. For much of the time Harry's driver duties required him to supply ammunition to gun batteries on the front line and to move artillery pieces when necessary. These tasks usually meant driving teams of six horses pulling heavy wagons or gun carriages. He is eventually appointed as a servant to Lieutenant (later Captain) Wigg and tried at one point to get a commission in the RAF, but (thankfully, as my own very existence probably depended on it) he is refused.

He is on leave when the war ends, but is required to go back. He grumbles, yet seems to go from club to cinema, to dance hall, to ball, playing piano or singing. He visits towns with colleagues (and girls) and is no longer sleeping under carts or in barns but in decent lodgings. My mother tells me that his fiancé, my future grandmother, was not at all happy about this given that most other men had already been demobbed, and that it was because of his value as a musician that he was kept on.

At Clayton Methodist Church organ 1949

LIST OF ILLUSTRATIONS

GLOSSARY

DHQ – District headquarters [?]
Estaminet – coffee house/smoking room
GS Wagon – General Service wagon
M & D – Medicine and duties
Piquet – sentry duty
QMS - Quartermaster Sergeant
RFA – Royal Field Artillery
TM - Trench Mortar
'W' – Winifred Crowther, Harry's future wife
WR – West Riding of Yorkshire
YM - YMCA

WAR RECORD

1915–1919

HARRY WESTERMAN

WAR RECORD

1915

Joined up at Valley Parade Barracks Oct 7/1915. in the 3/2 West Riding Royal Field Artillery (Territorial). Reg. No 3315. as a Driver.

" Did first Parade on Oct 12/1915 my 21st Birthday, at Valley Parade Barracks.

Oct 13. Played Soccer at Valley Parade for R.F.A. Scored a goal. Trial Match.

" 27 " " " " " " We won 2-0. Scored a goal.

Nov 1. Inoculated. 4 days off duty. Bed for 22 hrs.

" 2 Got out of bed. No pain.

" 8 Working at Recruiting Office Bridge St.

" 10 Played Soccer with R.F.A v Bfd Tradesmen, at Greenfield. Played right wing. Won 3-1.

" 12 Playing for concert at Khaki Club, Forster Square.

" 15 Barracks for Drill. Working over at Recruiting Office.

Dec 1 R.F.A Dance at Windsor Hall.

" 8 Working at Cleckheaton, Recruiting

" 9 " " Farsley & Calverly "

" 10 " " Idle "

" 15 At Riding School. Fell off horse. Riding bareback. Rather hurt.

" 17 Inoculated and vaccinated 2nd time. Stable duty at morning.

" 18 Arm very swollen and stiff.

" 20 Rather ill with the inoculation.

" 29 Riding School. Grooming and riding etc.

1916

Back end of Feb. or beginning of March left Bfd. for South Camp, Ripon.

In huts, not so bad.

Had a few leaves home, and W. came over there once.

Usual work while there such as drill stables every day etc.

Left Ripon in April for France.

Played in Football Match before, and got Footballers Knee very bad.

Went to station on a G.S. wagon.

Arrived Folkestone.

Left in the evening of April 12? 1916, on SS Victoria.

1915

Joined up at Valley Parade Barracks October 7 1915 in the 3/2 West Riding Royal Field Artillery (Territorial) Reg. No. 3315 as a Driver. Did first parade on October 12 1915, my 21st birthday, at Valley Parade Barracks.

Oct 13
Played soccer at Valley Parade for RFA. Scored a goal trial match.

Oct 27
Played soccer at Valley Parade for RFA. We won 2.0 Scored a goal.

Nov 1
Inoculated; 4 days off duty. Bed for 22 hours.

Nov 2
Got out of bed. No pain.

Nov 8
Working at Recruiting Office, Bridge Street

Nov 10
Played Soccer with RFA v Bradford Tradesmen at Greenfield. Played Right-wing. Won 3:1

Nov 12
Playing for concert at Khaki Club, Forster Square.

Nov 15
Barracks for drill, working over at Recruiting Office.

Dec 1
RFA Dance at Windsor Hall.

Dec 8
Working at Cleckheaton Recruiting.

Dec 9
Working at Farsley and Calverly Recruiting.

Dec 10
Working at Idle Recruiting.

Dec 15
At Riding School. Fell off horse riding bareback. Rather hurt.

Dec 17
Inoculated and vaccinated 2nd time. Stable duty at morning.

Dec 18
Arm very swollen and stiff.

Dec 20
Rather ill with the inoculation.

Dec 29
Riding School. Grooming and riding etc.

BILL'S LUCK.

First Coster; Well poor old Bill's gone.

Second Coster: (scornfully). "Poor, indeed! Luckiest bloke in the market. Couldn't touch nuffink wifout it turned to money. Insured 'is 'ouse — burned in a month. Insured 'isself agin' accidents, broke 'is arm first week. Joined the burial society last Toosday and now 'e's opped it "I call it luck!"

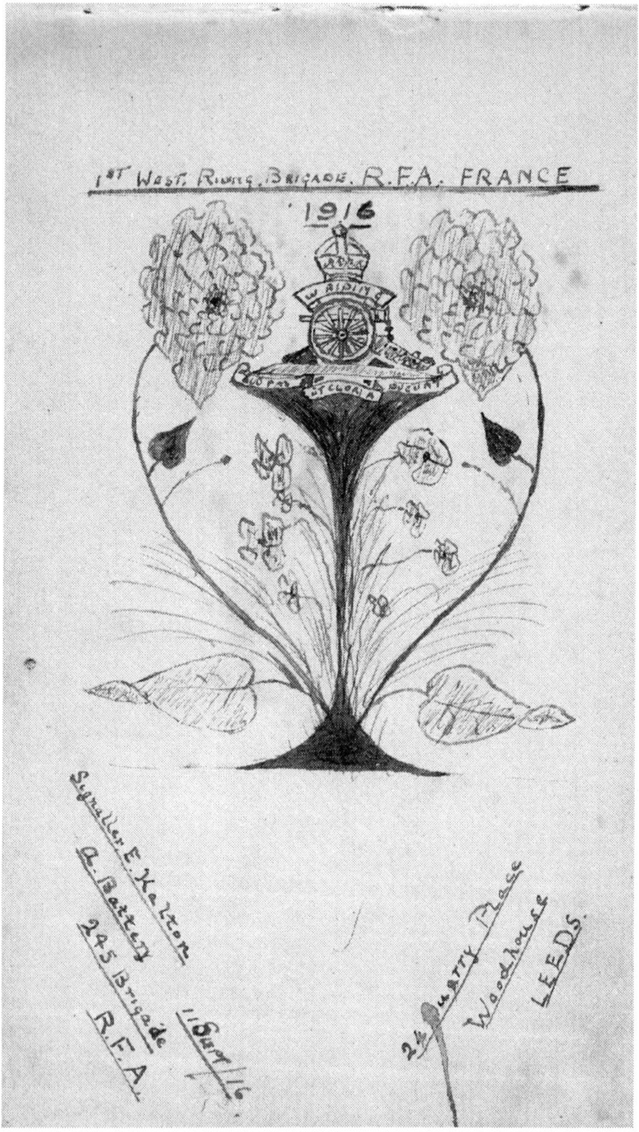
1st West Riding Brigade. R.F.A. FRANCE
1916
Signaller E. Kalton
A. Battery
245 Brigade
R.F.A.
11 Sept/16
24 Quarry Place
Woodhouse
LEEDS.

1916

Back end of Feb or beginning of March, left Bradford for South Camp, Ripon.
In huts, not so bad.
Had a few leaves home, and W. came over there once.
Usual work while there such as drill, stables every day etc.
Left Ripon in April for France.
Played in football match before, and got footballer's knee very bad.
Went to Station on a GS Wagon.
Arrived Folkestone.
Left in the evening of April 12? 1916 on *SS Victoria*.
Had a lovely and calm crossing.
Arrived Boulogne early morning.
Then to St Martin's Camp on hill Top. What a drag.
I had to be helped up there, my knee so very painful.
Medical exam next morning, and I was sent to hospital.
No 3 Canadian General (McGill) at Boulogne.
Stayed in bed there 11 days, then moved across to Nord Convalescent Camp and placed in "L" Company.
A very nice place and clean , with very good food.
Eventually stayed there about three months.
Had a job as storeman for the company; cushy.
Played piano for concerts at YMCA and for Officers' and Sergeants' Messes.
Quite a good time. Could go to town anytime.
Then sent to Havre or rather the camp at Harfleur, near Havre.
In tents there with the West Riding Division. Several Bradford boys there too.
All right. No 16 Camp.

1916 !

N.Tennant became a well-known cartoonist

Had heavy work there. Heaps of fatigues etc. of all descriptions.
Went for days at a time on fatigues to Havre docks to unload ships etc.
Very hard work and long hours.
Eventually after a time got a staff position as a pianist at No 14 Camp Cinema (YMCA) with orchestra which was very good. Well paid for it.
At Havre about 9 months.
Eventually, got a permanent pass for town and made good use of it.
Nov 11?
Owing to a mistake of a sergeant, I was eventually sent up the line along with more to the 255 Brigade RFA. 51st Division
Arrived at night at Acheaux Railhead after a journey of a long period.
Lost my pals and wandered about until day break. Very cold.
At last was put to "C" Battery, 255 Brigade RFA All Scotch. Very clannish.

After 2 days was sent up line as brakeman to guns at Maily-Mailly, just before taking of Beaumont Hamel.
Left Acheaux in a few days and transferred to "B" Battery and went to Bougincourt all in the mud, awful.
Guns were at Courcelette, near the Sugar Refinery.
Wagon lines at Bougincourt, and bad weather prevailed.
From lines we could see the fallen Virgin on Albert Cathedral, being near to Albert.
To guns we had to go through Albert and up the main Baupacme Road, turning down a little by-road just after leaving Pozieres.
In full view of enemy part way down this road and we were shelled often.
To get to the guns we had to go through mud and water which came up almost to the haunches of our horses. Some mud.
Anyhow near the end of December 1916 we left there and went on the "Trek" finally arriving at Grand Laviers, near Abbeville beginning of January. Bitterly cold weather just now.

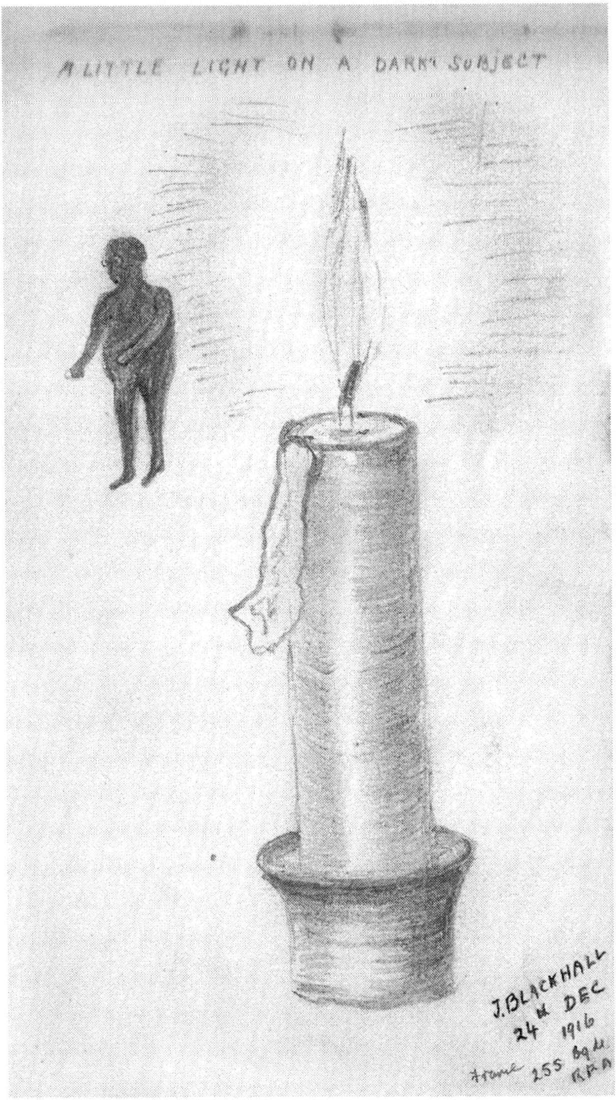
A LITTLE LIGHT ON A DARK SUBJECT
J. BLACKHALL
24 th DEC
1916
France
255 Bgde
RFA

1917.

Tommy. S'pose you've got a wife

THE HUN. Nein

Tommy. Nine! Blimy! Where's your Iron Cross

May 21/17.

1917

JANUARY

Jan 1

Had a day off except for water and feed. Most of the boys drunk. On piquet at night. Thankless job too.

Jan 2

Up line at 4 am. "Rally"on. Digging and making a Gun pit. All the sky lit up with dumps on fire etc. Fine sights.

Jan 3

Fine morning. Up line with wagon to take working party and bring them back.

Jan 4

Raining. Out exercising. Went to Fritz's Well. Off on "Trek". At Grand Laviers.

Jan 28

Very severe frost. In a barn.

Jan 29

Cold in the head, in bed early.

Jan 30

Went to army hut. Playing organ.

Jan 31

On piquet. Writing letters, Could hear rumble of guns.

FEBRUARY

Feb 7
At Conchy. Decent barn, but awful roads. Frosty.

Feb 8
Near Arras Roads bad, frosty. no tea ration. 10/- home, 2/- Dobson.

Feb 9
Nice Day. In estaminet having chips etc. Gramophone playing.

Feb 10
Beautiful day. Going to Trench Mortar working party.
left Marioncourt le Conte in Motor wagon for Arras.
Billeted in Calvary Barracks - Arras.

Feb 11
Misty. Nothing to do all day. No orders. Went to hear Gypsy Smith at YM . Arras. Met Mr Harrison of YM. Havre.

Feb 12
Thaw started. Up at 7.00 am. Working in communication trench. north of St Catherine, near Rocklincourt. Went to tea at YM in company with Gypsy Smith. 18 more men up from Battery for TM [Trench Mortar] working party.

Feb 13
Up at 8.00 am. Parade 9.00 am. Did not go to trenches after all.
Went to YM. Writing letters all the day, nearly.

Feb 14
Beautiful day. Enemy aircraft overhead. No parade for me all day.
In RGA Canteen. More aircraft over. Busy.

Feb 15
Beautiful day. Parade 9.30 am. Cleaning billets.

Feb 16
In trenches, 600 yards from front line trenches. Making TM positions. Hard and frosty going up but very muddy coming down. Raining a little. In Catholic Club playing piano at night.

Feb 17
Went sick. Bladder and throat. Got M & D, the Devil. Up line at 1.30 pm. Came back about 6.00 pm. Sloppy and muddy.

Feb 18
Went sick. Feet. Got M & D. The Devil take him. Raining. Newman sent to hospital. Up to trenches. Plenty of mud.

Feb 19
Parade at 9.30 am. Dismissed. Parade 4.40 pm. Began to be ill Stayed in bed. Pains in legs and head. Awful.

Feb 20
Reported sick. Sent to hospital. Afternoon at ½ Highland FDS. My temperature 100° F. Decent Hospital. Hautrevenes.

Feb 21
Raining. Sent to 30th C Clearing Station, Aubigny, on stretcher in motor. In Ward, Bed 53. Decent place. Had slight Trench Fever.

Feb 22
Raining. Still in bed temp 98° F.

Feb 23
Still in bed.

Feb 24
Still in CCS. Got up in afternoon.

Feb 25
Fine. Out in town a while.

Feb 26
Still at CCS. Germans retreating on Somme.

Feb 27
Still at CCS. Met Bradford fellow Taylor. Had a bath for a change.

Feb 28
Walked back to Arras Calvary Barracks about 16/18 kg with full kit. Newman back at battery. Fellows left Arras. Walked to Anzin to guns. Rode back at night in DAC GS wagon to Frevent Capelle then walked to Augbigny CCS. Slept there in office.

MARCH

Mar 1
Breakfast at CCS. Then met Ration Wagon at Station.
Came on that in afternoon to Ourton to Battery on rest.
Decent billets.
The usual while here. Stables parade etc.

Mar 9
Left Ourton, 10.00 am. Very cold, snowing and blowing of course.
Arrived Frevent- Capelle about 3.00 pm. Put big marquees up all right.

Mar 10
Misty and raining. Half day off. Newman goes to TM's.
Up line at 4.00 pm, with G S wagon also with ammunition.
Went to Arras at night. Back 11.30 pm. Late scholar.

Mar 11
Hot in morning. Slap dashing marquees. Rain in afternoon.
Walk to Acq. at night. Half day off. Heavy rain at night.

Mar 12
Another bath and a change in Frevent-Capelle.

Mar 13
Up line with ammunition. Loading ammunition until 12.00 am.

Bradford fellows arrive in Camp viz, Gardner, Williamson. Gardner put in my sub section F.

Mar 14
Raining in morning but cleared up. Horse lines in a mess. Took horse to forge.

Mar 15
Nice morning. Up line with ammunition. On piquet at night. Had last turn 2:00 am to 6:00 am.

Mar 16
Decent day. Harness cleaning.

Mar 17
Lovely day. Half day off. Playing football. Stayed in night.

Mar 18
Nice day. Went to Frevilles Wood for wood. Back at 2:00 pm Playing football afterwards.

Mar 19
Windy and dull. Heavy rain and the blooming tent leaks.

Mar 20
Raining. Loading ammunition. Pay at 1.30 pm. Cheers. Lost some playing Crown and Anchor.

Mar 21
Better day but rather cold. Up line with ammunition.

Mar 22
Snow at night.

Mar 23
Snow and very cold. Up line with ammunition.

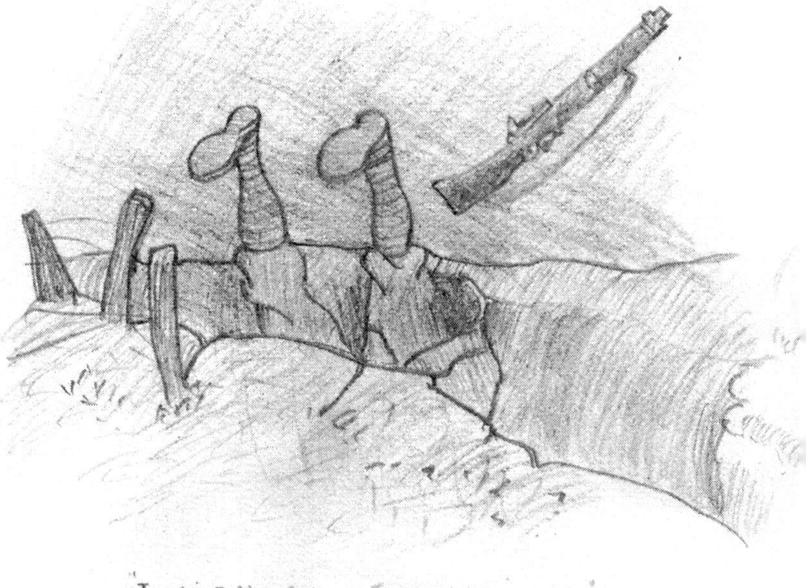

"I got into the German Trench right enough"

Mar 24
Fine but cold.

Mar 25
Fine day. Stayed in at night, writing.

Mar 26
Heavy rain. Driving with ammunition. No Ammunition wanted up line.

Mar 27
Dull and fine. No ammunition wanted. Mr Gadie passed by.

Mar 28
Fine and crisp day. No line. Commenced 6.30 pm parade stables.

Mar 29
Raining.

Mar 30
Taken ill at morning. Went over to see Bradford Brigade on Angin Common.
Feeling sick etc.

Mar 31
Nice day. Went sick. Sent to hospital with Tonsillitis - Hautrevenes, Ward 2.
Brother Tom came to see me I heard. Gargling. Thunder and rain at night.

APRIL

Apr 1
Nice day. At Hautevenes. Left H for Coucourt. DRS. Got there for tea. Raining.

Apr 2
In DRS. Snow and cold. In bed.

Apr 3
Snowing heavily. In bed. Had throat painted with iodine. Sardines for tea. Fine again.

Apr 4
Decent day. In bed morning. Got up in afternoon. Gramophone in ward. Had a short walk.

Apr 5
Up again. Lovely day. Had a walk.

Apr 6
Left DRS. Raining. Had a good feed. Arrived at Savy Con Camp. Terrible place. Bombardment going on.

Apr 7
Fine day. Went back to battery.

Apr 8
Fine day. Push commences. Cavalry moving.

Apr 9
Brother Tom wounded. Took our guns forward to Rocklincourt. Out all day working hard. Moved wagon lines to Angin.

Apr 10
Up line again.

Apr 11
Moved guns to St Nicholas. Awful sights near by.

Apr 12
Moved forward over ground captured. Lots of dead.

Apr 13
Busy.

Apr 14
Moved guns forward again. Saw some German guns. Awful place.

Apr 18
Up line with rations . Shelling.

Apr 19
Moved back to Angin from Laurient-Blanchy.

Apr 20
Up line at 2:00 am. Back at 8:00 am. Nice day.

Apr 21
Nice day. Got paid. Went to Maroul on cycle.

Apr 22
Beautiful day. Heavy firing on. Grooming. Went to Arras on cycle. Heaps of Troops there.

Apr 23
Beautiful day. Moved at 8:00 am forward. Advance. Up line to bring guns out and take forward. Saw heaps of wounded. Shell missed us by few yards. Back safely.

Apr 24
Beautiful day. Enemy dropping bombs and shelling very near us. Put "Bivvy" up. Big guns going.

Apr 25
Germans counter attacking. Jones wounded. 2 horses wounded. Dull morning. Stayed in writing at night.

Apr 26
Nice day. Going up line at 5.00pm. Keith wounded.
Heavy shelling on road.
Luckily our team not shelled. Home quite safely.

Apr 27
Nice day. On cycle to Headquarters up line.
Back at 2:00 pm, stayed in at night.

Apr 28
Fine day. Every team up line. Germans advanced, a little.
Going up line at 2:00 pm.

Apr 29
Beautiful and very hot. Working and walking without tunics. Harness cleaning in afternoon. Gramophone going at night.

Apr 30
Beautiful and warm. Teams up line. Went up line with rations.
Shelled. Saw German Red Devil aeroplane over our guns.
16th Bradford Pals in St Catherine.

MAY

May 1
Lovely day. German 'plane' brought down on the Common.
Turned turtle then righted itself and made good landing.

May 2
Lovely day. Went to baths again.
Lights out, enemy dropping bombs here.
Bombardment begins.

May 3
Lovely day. Bombardment still on and very heavy. Teams up line.
Shelled. Saw G Owen at night about 9.30 pm on way back.

May 4
Lovely day. No teams out. Paid 15 francs. Gas helmets ready.
Big dump at St Catherine struck by shell. Tremendous bursts, burning all night. Down to hear Pals Band at St Catherine.

May 5
Lovely day. Dump burnt out. Half day off. Harness inspection in morn. Went to Pals at night. Met G Owen, Palfrayman etc. Then to see Lt Clary Gadie. Saw Edmonson too.

May 6
Rather cold and windy. Custard for breakfast. Some "do". Went to hear Pals Band. 2 playing alternately.

May 7
Nice day, but rain at night. Went to hear Band again.

May 8
Raining and sloppy. On piquet of course. Went up line at night.

May 9
Nice day. Took horses to graze. Stayed in at night writing.

May 10
Went up line, in afternoon. Shelled going up Death Valley. 2 Tanks passed over Common. Looked very funny. Horses nervous.

May 11
Nice day. Very hot. Grazing horses. Clean harness until 8:30 pm.

May 12
Very hot. Stables in morn. Half day. Up line about 5:00 pm. Very quiet

May 13
Fine and warm. Grazing in afternoon. Writing at night. Rain.

May 14
Fine again. Gardner up line. Heavy rain in afternoon. Pool of water in our "bivvy". Scooping out. My horse "Darkie" has colic.

TIT-BITS OF THE WAR

FROM FRENCH LITANY OF THE TRENCHES

"NOTHING TO WORRY ABOUT"

You have two alternatives: Either you are mobilized or you are not. If not, you have nothing to worry about.

If you are, you have two alternatives. Either you are in camp or at the front. If you are in camp, you have nothing to worry about.

If you are at the front, you have two alternatives. Either you are in reserve or you are in the fighting line. If you are in reserve you have nothing to worry about.

If you are in the fighting line, you have two alternatives, Either you scrap or you don't. If you don't you have nothing to worry about.

If you do, you have two alternatives. Either you get hurt or you are badly hurt. If slightly, you have nothing to worry about.

If badly, you have two alternatives, either you recover or you don't.

If you recover, you have nothing to worry about.

If you don't, and have followed my advice clear through, you have done with worry for ever.

May 15
Dull morning. Grazing in afternoon.

May 16
Dull and raining. Later cold. Up at 3:00 am. Up line, 12 wagons. Shelling roads and gun position. Got splashed with mud caused by a shell bursting near by. Two horses wounded. Back safely. Saw the Scottie I met at Boulogne Con Camp.

May 17
Raining. Up line again with ammunition at 7.00am. No shelling. Went to hear Pals Band at night.

May 18
Bright morning. Grazing in afternoon. I pinched a fine horse.

May 19
Nice day. Went on my new horse, "Dumphie", to Aubigny. Good time, got back 11:40 pm.

May 20
Church service in morning, Nice day. Divisional Band playing here in afternoon. Horse jumping practise. Reading at night.

May 21
Reported sick. Gums very sore. Rained a little. Grazing in afternoon. Writing and reading at night.

May 22
Raining almost all day, cleared at night. A WR [West Riding] fellow, DCM arrives in my shack. Nice chap.

May 23
Very hot and fine. Playing football.

May 24
Nice day. Very hot. Playing football in evening. Shopping.

May 25

Very hot. Grazing in morning and afternoon. German "plane" over at night, dropping bombs in Anzin.

May 26

Very hot. Grazing. Half day off. Writing.

May 27

Lovely day. Up line at 3:00 am to bring damaged gun out of position.

May 28

German plane over again in early morning. Beautiful day.
Full marching order parade of teams at 2.30 pm. Major's inspection.
Went to hear band afterwards.

May 29

Fine day. Applied for position of Battery Clerk. No mail.

May 30

Fine morning, but some rain in afternoon. Grazing. Harness cleaning.
Went to Arras. Had a good look around. Back at 10.00pm. No mail.

May 31

Nice morning. Inspection Parade. Water and feed at 8:30 pm.
Harness cleaning. No mail.

JUNE

Jun 1

Lovely day. Enemy "plane" over head. Heaps of shrapnel falling here.
Paid. Mail arrives.

Jun 2

Lovely day, Wagons painted. Harness cleaned. Inspection by Colonel.
Our team of all blacks won first prize. Cigs all round.
Went for a swim in River Scarfe. Strong current. Writing at night.

Jun 3
Lovely day. Full Brigade Service. I was in choir. Half day off. Planes over again at night. Dropping bombs.

Jun 4
Lovely day. Up line at 4:00 am with ammunition. Shelled with 8 inch. Forsyth killed and one wounded. Shells dropping too near to be healthy.Harness cleaning in afternoon. Playing in cricket match in evening. First man in scored 3.

Jun 5
Very hot and fine. Planes over again. Blooming nuisance. Jimmy Forsyth's funeral in morning. Buried just here. Grazing in afternoon.

Jun 6
Very hot. Up line as orderly to headquarters. Advanced a little. Saw two prisoners. On piquet. Luck again. Heavy rain and thunder. On first turn for a change 6:00 pm till 10:00 pm.

Jun 7
Heavy and close. Reported sick with tonsils. Excused duty one day. Raining a little. Writing at night.

Jun 8
Fine but dull. Exercise horses. Heavy bombardment.

Jun 9
Fine but dull. Half day off. Listened to Band. Could not find Pals. Must have gone.

Jun 10
Fine and warm. Exercise horses. Half day off. Church Service. In choir.

Jun 11
Heavy rain. Almost flooded out. Cleared at night. Writing.

Jun 12
Fine and hot. German plane brought down here. Had a walk at night after writing.

Jun 13
Nice morning. Teams up line. I did not go. Went to Arras.

Jun 14
Lovely day. Harness cleaning. Writing at night.

Jun 15
Lovely day. Paid. No mail.

Jun 16
Very hot. Half day off.

Jun 17
Very hot. Service. In Choir. Had a talk with the Chaplain. Playing cricket v RNMC 5.00pm. First man in.

Jun 18
Raining part time. Left Anzin for Acq . Left Anzin 7:00 pm to go up line for gun. Arrived Acq 2.00am. Shelling with 8in in bottom of Death Valley

Jun 19
Missed first parade. Raining. Stables. Harness cleaning . Went to Hautevnes at night.

Jun 20
Raining a little. Exercise and harness cleaning. Went to Acq. and Frevent-Capelle at night, then on piquet. Very dark night. Missed the 8:30 pm parade.

Jun 21
Raining in afternoon. Parade 4:00 am. Marching order. Round roads. No mail.

And Still They Ask

In a well known military hospital in the South of England the patients grew weary of answering ?s on their experiences at the Front and the following placard is now prominently displayed:—

Visitors are given a hearty welcome but please do not ask the following ?s.

1/ are you wounded?
2/ Did it hurt?
3/ Which hurt most – going in or reverse?
4/ How did you know you were wounded?
5/ Did the shell hit you?
6/ Did you see any Germans?
7/ Do you want to go back?
8/ How many did you kill.

By request
THE PATIENTS

amgen [illegible] June 7/17

Jun 22
Returned from march at 6:00 am. Raining part of day. Exercise etc. Time in afternoon. Cold. Water and feed 8:30 pm.

Jun 23
Lovely day. Reveille 5:30 am. Marching order. Driving Drill. Driving between the pegs. Half day off. Went for a walk.

Jun 24
Lovely day. Half day off for sports and show. Church Parade. Went to see aerodrome at night. "B" Battery, won jumping, driving, harness wagon, in fact first in everything.

Jun 25
Half day off.

Jun 26
In Acq.

Jun 27
Route March.

Jun 28
Raining heavily. Smoker [?] at Acq "Empire". Singing and playing, sung "Perfect Day" and "They didn't believe me". Very good. A good feed. Finished at 11:15 pm.

Jun 29
Dull but fine. Exercised horses. In Acq at night.

Jun 30
Heavy Rain. In Acq. Packing up at night.

JULY

Jul 1
Dull and dark. Up at 1:30 am. Left Acq at 4:10 am. Arrived St Michel, near St Pol 11:00 am. Stalls for horses and barns for us in St Pol.

Jul 2

Nice morning. Parade 9:00 am. Warm. Went for guns. In St Pol at night. Reveille 12:00 pm leave 2:30 am. Very little sleep. Passed Pernes. Arrived 10:00 pm near Lillers.

Jul 3

Arrived 10:00 am. Sleeping in a wood at Amettes.

Jul 4

Arrived Boesghem, near Aire. Went to see Aire Cathedral. Fine place.

Jul 5

Left Boesghem 5:30 am. Arrived Staples 8:00 am. Fine place. English spoken a lot. Went in church to try organ. Fine. Good wagon lines. Slept in a field.

Jul 6

Lovely day. Left Staples 4:30 am, passed Cassel. Wagon line near Staerwaden. Fine church there. Arrived 9:00 am. Good time here. Slept in the open.

Jul 7

Hot day. Left Staerwaden arrived Vlamarterge outside Popperinghe. In Church Army hut playing piano. Shelling. Planes over. Heavy shelling and bombing at night. Raining. Awful place for nerves.

Jul 8

Still raining. Parade. Shelling all day. Went to service at Army hut. Played for service.

Jul 9

Dull and cold. Raining. Exercise. Shelling again.

Jul 10

Nice morning. Exercise. Shelling near here again. Went to Army Hut.

Jul 11
Nice morning. Shelling again. Exercise......

Jul 12
Fine day. Shelling wagon lines. 1 killed several wounded. "Stand by" horses order.

Jul 13
Moved out wagon lines. Two shells burst very near. Crouching under our horses for cover. Ammunition up line. Two horses killed.

Jul 14
Raining. Going up line at 9:00 pm with ammunition. Six teams. Went to gun position. Heavy shelling. Lost the others, walked back. Soaking wet. Arrived in camp 5:30 am on my own. Went to bed until my clothes dried.

Jul 15
Turned out fine. My clothes dried well. Stayed in bed all day. On piquet. Got off it. Thank goodness. Had a jolly good supper of potatoes, peas etc. gathered in the fields near by.

Jul 16
Lovely day. Usual routine. Going up line with ammunition. Driving wheel 9:30 pm . Back at 3:00 am. Shelling very near and gas floating about.

Jul 17
Lovely day. Morning in bed.

Jul 18
Raining almost all day. Up line with packs at 2:00 pm. Back at 7:00 pm. Very quiet up line. Rotten job with packs.

Jul 19
Dull day. Late on Parade for once. Put on dung fatigue for one and half hours at night. Shell dropped and wrecked part of army hut.

Jul 20
Warm but dull. Up line with a gun at 2:00 pm. Shelling, a rough time coming back. Back at 10:30 pm.

Jul 21
Lovely day. Exercise etc. Half day off.

Jul 22
Lovely day. "C" Battery gun team wiped out going up line. High bursts over lines. Lots of killed on roads.

Jul 23
Lovely day. Exercise etc.

Jul 24
(Left blank)

Jul 25
Raining. Paid 20 francs. Went to Popperinghe for bath. Saw Metcalfe. No mail. Went to RGA to see Thompson.

Jul 26
Fine Day. Bombardment on. Usual harness cleaning, No mail. On piquet. Writing.

Jul 27
Fine day. Usual routine. Rumour of Germans retreating.

Jul 28
Fine and hot. Half day off. Went to Popperinghe. Went in church. Good time.

Jul 29
Heavy rain. Service in morning. In choir. Late on parade. Walk at night.

Jul 30
Rain in morning. All horses clipped. Went to Church Army Hut.

Jul 31
Dull. Drizzling. Reveille 3:00 am. Up line with gun team at 4:00 am. Advance. Infantry over at 4.06 am and advancing. Took St Julien. We advanced too. Thousands of prisoners coming down.

AUGUST

Aug 1
Heavy rain all day and night. Road flooded, river flooded. Jocks wading through. Advance stopped. A fellow here wading barelegged to recover his saddle. In "bivvy" all day.

Aug 2
Ground a quagmire. Up line with packs but turned back conditions so very bad.

Aug 3
Raining. Out in mud, exercising. Out in rain with packs in afternoon. Up line at night again with ammunition. Terrible. Wet through.

Aug 4
Three years of it! Raining heavily.

Aug 5
Fine day. Up line.

Aug 6
Fine day.

Aug 7
Fine day. Up line to new forward position at St Julien with ammunition. Up at 1.00am back at 5.00am.

Aug 8
Fine day. Up line with ammunition. On piquet. Terrible storm at night. Thunder and lightening. Always seem to hit a bad night for being on piquet. Luck!

Aug 9
Fine day. Up line with packs.

Aug 10
Fine day. Rain at night. Up line at night with wagons.
Very little shelling.

Aug 11
Fine morning. 60 packs up line. Went to Popperinghe for gun.
Back at 5.30pm. Had a feed in Popp. Rain at night.

Aug 12
Fine morning but dull. Up line with packs. Heavily shelled. Enemy balloons up. Saw German's old trenches. Lots killed. Got back safely. Enemy plane brought balloon down here.

Aug 13
Nice day. Half day off.

Aug 14
Heavy rain at intervals. Half day off. No mail.

Aug 15
Raining most of day. Up line at 6:00 pm until 11:00 pm. Bombardment started. A-team wiped out.

Aug 16
Decent day. Advancing on our left. Prisoners coming down.
Up with ammunition in morning. No mail. Shelling lines.

'What the fish said'

Aug 17
Fine Day. Up line at 8:15 am. Two journeys, back at 3:45 pm. Shelling. Several horses and men wounded. Planes in search light.

Aug 18
Fine day. Did not go up line. Thank goodness.

Aug 19
Aeroplanes over. Bombing. Up line at 1:00 am with wagons. 6 horse. Daylight when there. Back at 8:00 am. Shelling near us. 1200 rounds of ammunition taken up. I fell and horse trod on my knee, on sleeper track. "Planes" over again at night.

Aug 20
Nice day. Up line again. Quiet. Planes over. One brought down here. Bombing again. Feeling sick with my knee.

Aug 21
Nice day. Plenty of enemy planes over. Harness cleaning etc.

Aug 22
Nice and hot. Up line with wagons at 1:00 am. Quiet. Rally commenced when at the guns. Back 7:30 am. Parade 2:00 pm. German "plane" brought down.

Aug 23
Dull day. Teams up line again. Did not go.

Aug 24
Decent day with showers. Up line at 1:00 am. Up line again in afternoon with rations. Very quiet.

Aug 25
Decent day. Harness inspection in afternoon. Our sub "F" Second Prize.

Aug 26
Nice day. Up line at 1:00 am. Shelling very near. Half day off. Heavy rain at night.

Aug 27
Heavy rain, cleared a little later. Up line to old position for shell cases. Bombarding again.

Aug 28
Raining. Up line again at 6.00 pm. Quiet up line. Place flooded again. Battery commandeered a canteen.

Aug 29
Rain at intervals. On piquet 10 - 2 am.

Aug 30
Boys up line at 3:00 am, did not go. Fine day but dull.

Aug 31
Rain at times. Up line at 3:00 am. Very quiet. Bright moonlight night and of course planes over bombing. A-Battery in next field, 1 horse killed and 2 men wounded.

SEPTEMBER

Sept 1
Beautiful at 6.00 am. Planes over again. Drill later.

Sept 3
Beautiful and warm. Played on Scottish Church piano, very fine.

Sept 4
Beautiful and warm. Plenty of work on lines. Pay.

Sept 5
Hot. Up line at 3.00 am packs. One of our planes brought down.

Sept 6
Very hot day. No ammunition wanted. Heavy rain at night.

Sept 7
Flooded again.

Sept 9
Fine day. Inspection of harness. Looks fine.

Sept 10
Fine day and hot. Up line at 7.30 am with mess cart for Officers' kit. Half day off.

Sept 12
Fine day. Half day off. Went to Scottish Church to honour W's birthday. Daylight bombing raid.

Sept 13
Fine day. Dull at night rain. Digging ourselves in, made big trench outside "bivvy".

Sept 14
Decent morning. Wagons up line. Going for coal to Popp.

Sept 15
Nice day. Up line at 3.00 am with wagons. Harness cleaning etc.

Sept 16
Very hot and fine. Harness inspection. "Planes" over again.

Sept 17
Fine day. Up line at 3.00 am with wagons. Double journey. Quiet. More teams up line in afternoon. Did not go.

Sept 18
Dull day. Up line at 4.00 am with packs. 2 journeys. Half day off. Pay.

Sept 19
Raining. Half day off.

Sept 20
Fine day. Up line in morning. Advance. 700 prisoners.

Sept 21
Up line with wagons in afternoon. Counter attacks. Back at dark. Planes over. We were bombed by a plane coming back.

Sept 22
Fine day.

Sept 23
Fine day. Bdr Wilkinson and horse both wounded with bomb.

Sept 24
Fine day. Up line at 4.00 am with packs. Foggy. Heavy shelling. Gas shells. A horse killed. Back safely at 1.30pm. Baths in afternoon.

Sept 25
Fine day. Up with packs again. A & C batteries going up to forward positions cancelled.

Sept 26
Dull morning. Bombarded at night. Packs to new position at night. I did not go.

Sept 27
Fine day. Up line with rations in afternoon. Moonlight night bombing raid. Packs up line again. "A" Battery in next field, a mess. About 30 horses killed and wounded with bombs. Terrible sights.

Sept 28
Fine and hot. Packs up again. I did not go.

Drawing of a woman by Harry, from his autograph book.

Sept 29
Fine day. Up line at 4.00 am. Took gun forward to position. Fairly quiet.

Sept 30
4 going on leave. Went up line to forward positions with packs. "Jerry" over.

OCTOBER

Oct 1
Lovely day.

Oct 2
Down at Popp

Oct 3
LEAVE. Left early morning from Vlamenturge for Popp.

Oct 4
In England. Called to see Tom in Hospital, in London

Oct 7
2 years in army. 3rd day of proficiency pay.

Oct 12
Birthday. Alhambra. Formby.

Oct 13
Leave finished. Rotten luck. Leave Bradford, Midland Railway at 10.45 pm. W saw me off.

Oct 14
Arrived London 8.30 am. Day here. Saw Tom again, Stayed YM.

Oct 15
Left London 7.00 am. Folkestone at 9.00 am. Arrived Boulogne 10.40 am Then to Rest Camp No 5. Leaving at 10.00 pm for Popp. Calm crossing.

Oct 16
Arrive Popp 11.15 am. Got paid. Dinner in Popp.

Oct 17
Fine day but cold. Coming out of action. Popp at night.

Oct 18
On lines. In team for guns. In Popp at night.

Oct 19
Dull day. Entrained near Popp. Left lines 10.30 am, entrained at 4.00 pm, left at 6.00 pm.

Oct 20
Arrived Acheaux (Somme) at 10.00 am. Staying a while. Fine day.

Oct 22
Acheaux. Concert in YM by RFC.

Oct 25
Concert by D Battery in YM.

Oct 26
Concert by A Battery in YM.

Oct 28
Church Service in Y M. ½ day off.

Oct 29
Paid out . Beautiful night. Balmorals and Band arrive.

Oct 30
Raining nearly all day. Writing at night.

NOVEMBER

Nov 3
Left Acheaux at 8.00 am. Arrived Boiry St Martin 3.00 pm. Went to Y.M.

Nov 4
Reveille 5.30 am. Parade 6.00 am. Dull morning. Parade again 9.00 am.

Nov 5
At Y M. Concert party.

Nov 6
Raining. Left Boiry St Martin 6.30 am. Arrived at Acheaux 12.30 pm. ½ day off. In cafe.

Nov 7
Usual. Acheaux.

Nov 8
Usual.

Nov 9
Usual. Heavy Rain.

Nov 10
Usual. Heavy Rain.

Nov 11
Church service in YM. Nice day. Pay.

Nov 12
Usual. Writing at night.

Nov 13
Nice day. Day off from Battery. Battery concert in YM Acheaux. Playing and singing "Perfect Day" , "Thank you God for sleep". Good time.

Nov 14
Nice Day. Left Acheaux 4.15 pm, travelling all night. Arrived Coucelles 10.30 pm Via Baupaume. In tents.

Nov 15
Nice morn. Reveille 7.30 am. 8.00 am Parade. Grooming, Harness cleaning. Left Coucelles, via Baupeume. Arrived Bulling court at 8.30 pm. In huts.

Nov 16
Reveille 7.00 am, Breakfast 8.00 am, Parade 8.15 am, leave Bulling court. Harnessed up, but unharnessed again 6.30 pm. 12.00 to 3.00 on piquet.

Nov 17
Fine morning, leave Bulling court at 4.30 pm. Arrived at Bus 6.30pm In "bivvys", very dark, guns gone into action.

Nov 18
Fine. Parade 8.30 am. Put "bivvy" up. Water at Lechelle. Writing at night.

Nov 19
Fine. Usual Parade at 6.30 am.

Nov 20
Advance north of Baupaume. Guns in action in Metz Wood. Advance, guns to Graincourt. Two days "stand to".

Nov 21
"Standing by", moved guns forward again. Slept in Flesquires.

Nov 22
Wagon lines passed German trench at Flesquires. Lots of dead on both sides.Tanks smashed up and men burnt. Guns captured. Some awful sights of dead. German Officer made a stand here with gun and knocked out several tanks etc. Eventually bayonneted several times by Jocks.

Nov 23
Took Fontain Castan and Graincourt. Advance again. Could watch the "barrage" from wagon line and see Cambrai easily. Cavalry going up. Terrible battle at Fontain and Bourlon Wood. Could see from our lines.

Nov 24
Pretty hot on every side.

Nov 25
Fine day but cold. Moved wagon lines further back, near Ribecourt. Plenty of mail for me.

Nov 26
Fine day, cold. Usual. Ammunition up line.

Nov 27
Raining heavily. Bombing early. Guards gone up line.

Nov 28
Up line with ammunition at night. Heavy bombard at night.

Nov 29
Fine day.

Nov 30
Heavy counter attack by Germans, eventually driven back. Up to guns three times at night.

DECEMBER

Dec 1
Fine day. ½ day off. Shelling near at night.

Dec 2
Fine day.

Dec 8
On piquet. Reginaldo and Dipple both wounded. Horses killed.

Dec 9
Frosty then rain. To dump for ammunition. Heavy shelling.

Dec 10
Lovely day. Moved in sections A & B. I went on G S wagon to new gun position and wagon line at Harlincourt. Gun position at Doignes.

Dec 11
Frost and thaw. C & D subs. moved.

Dec 12
Fine day. E & F subs. move to Harlincourt. New horse for me.

Dec 13
Fine day. Stables.

Dec 14
Rain a little. Left Harlincourt. Arrived at Fremicourt about dinner time. Plenty of canteens here.

Dec 19
Playing piano at Fremicourt Cinema.

Dec 20
Cinema.

Dec 22
Lovely day. Up line at 6.20 am.

Dec 23
Nice day. Frosty. On piquet. Bombing lines. Two horses wounded.

Dec 24
Rain and frost. To Baupaume at 5.30 am for Remounts. Back at 2.00 pm. Roads in awful state.

Dec 25
Snow. Day off.

Drawing by Harry, from his autograph book

Dec 26
Lovely day. Snow fairly thick. Lovely moonlight night.

Dec 27
Nice day. Snow on roads. Very bad going. Up line with ammunition at 5.30 am.

Dec 28
Decent day.

Dec 29
Decent day. Paid out 25F. ½ day off. Writing.

Dec 30
Church Parade 9.00 am. ½ day off. Heavy "rally" on.

Dec 31
Decent day. Had a festal "beano" in a barn nearby. Good rum rations, crackers, fruit, nuts, cigs, etc. "Decent do"

VON FALKENHAUSSEN.

1918

JANUARY

Jan

1 At Cinema Fremicourt.

Jan 3

Fine Day. On piquet. 1st turn. Sgt Major Brookes leaves for D Battery.

Jan 4

Nice day. At Cinema "Charlie at the Bank".

Jan 5

Decent but dull. ½ day off. Playing football with Battery v 3b Labour Co. We lost 2.1. Couldn't get in Cinema at night.

Jan 6

Nice day but very cold. ½ day off. Cinema at night. Crowded. Stayed to sing.

Jan 7

Raining and sloppy. No mail.

Jan 8

Snowing, freezing. Very slippery. Stayed in at night. No mail.

Jan 9

Nice morning. Cold, slippery. Raining and thaw later. No mail.

Jan 10

Raining, Cinema at night. Writing. No mail.

Jan 11
Raining. Sloppy. Received Gum boots from W. No letters. No water for horses in morning.

Jan 12
Dull. ½ day off. Mail arrived. With army chaplain.

Jan 13
Estaminet. No mail. Usual.

Jan 14
Heavy rain. On piquet, of course.

Jan 15
Showery. Singing at concert at YM.

Jan 16
Singing at Y M concert. Also playing "Larboard Watch" Duet with Youngson, went fine.

Jan 17
Guns now at Beaumetz le Cambrai.

Jan 18
Some rain. In Y M playing. Lantern lecture on "Modern Photography". Good.

Jan 19
Raining at night. Up line with G S wagon until 4.00 pm. No mail. Called at Cinema. Concert at Y M.

Jan 20
Dull. Church Parade 10.15 am. Teams up line to move ammunition. I did not go. In YM to service. Sang a hymn as a solo.

Jan 21
Raining. Up line for ammunition at 9.00 am, back at 1.30 pm. Shelling our. 9.2s

Jan 25
Out of action. Arrive at St Ledger, near Authie.

Jan 27
Fine Day. ½ day off. Playing football with B team, lost 3.2.

Jan 28
Beautiful Spring Day. Driving drill etc. in morning. Harness cleaning, in afternoon also stables.

Jan 29
½ day off.

FEBRUARY

Feb 1
Heavy frost.

Feb 2
Lovely day. Harness inspection. Lt Harrison left section treat to a pint of beer for man with best harness. Went to Authie in afternoon to see Chaplain. Writing afterward.

Feb 3
Nice day. Walked to Authie in afternoon. Had tea there. Left St Ledger at 4.00 pm, arrived Authie 5.30pm. Left Authie at 8.30 pm arrived St Ledger at 10.15 pm. Paid 10F hence the visit out.

Feb 4
Not feeling well. Missed 1st Parade. Stables in morn. Harness in afternoon. On piquet.

Feb 5
Nice day. Battery concert at Authie. Lt Harrison very good. Good concert.

Feb 6
Lovely day. ½ day off. Kicked with a mule in morning so could not play football. B Battery won 2.0. Writing.

Feb 8
Raining.

Feb 9
Fine day. B Battery lost in cuptie with D Battery. 6.1. Paid 20F.

Feb 10
Paid a visit to Doullens, on horseback. Very nice trip. I took my horse "Dumphy".

Feb 12
Fine day. Left St Leger 10.00 am. Arrived Bourgincourt at 4.00 pm. Memories of 1916.

Feb 13
Raining. In huts at Bourgincourt. Gramophone in hut.

Feb 14
Dull and rain. On piquet. Again my luck. Reveille at 4.45 am. Move off 8.30 am. Left Bourgincourt, via Albert to Fremicourt, once again. 24–26 kilo "trek". Arrived at Fremincourt 4.00 pm. In huts. All right. Stables too, but very muddy. Y M at night.

Feb 15
Dull day. Lecture in YM at 6.30 pm on "Ideal Government" by Prof Childes of Reading University. Very good.

Feb 16
Very cold and frosty. ½ day off. Went to concert at Y M. "Taysiders". Concert stopped on account of heavy bombing.

Feb 17
Much bombing again. Trampled on by my big horse, right on my big toe. Burst it open and made me lame.

Feb 18
Cold. Paraded sick with my toe. Dressing and duty but not to do much walking. Bombing again at night.

Feb 19
Cold and frost. Full battery on fatigues to R E dump at Beaugny, C R A Inspection. I missed the lot by parading with toe for dressing.

Feb 20
Cold, frost. Sick parade again, got light duty. Harness cleaning at 2.00 pm.

Feb 22
At YMCA.

Feb 23
Cinema at night.

Feb 24
Raining a little. Up line with rations. Sports being held outside huts.

Feb 25
Windy and rain. Went to baths. Had medical inspection for commission. On piquet.

Feb 26
Nice morning. In YM.

Feb 27
Nice morning. Bradford man named Gordon Bowling in Battery.

Feb 28
In Y M singing and playing.

MARCH

Mar 1

Nice day but cold. Major's inspection at 2.00 pm. Men brushing each other with their "dandys".

Mar 2

Awful blizzard. Stayed in.

Mar 3

Snow and freezing. At service at Y M.

Mar 4, 5, 6

Not on duty.

Mar 8

Sports. Racecourse behind huts. Jumping etc. Lt Martin hurt at last jump. Fine affair.

Mar 9

Fine day. ½ day off. On piquet. Pictures in afternoon.

Mar 10

Fine day. ½ day off. General march past before C R A of 2nd Brigade. We had to groom, water and feed in our gas masks. Cinema at night, "Good and Bad Men".

Mar 13

Lovely day. Commenced servants duties to Lt Wigg at Artillery, Headquarters at Fremincourt.

Mar 14

Lovely day.

Mar 15

Lovely day.

Lieutenant Wigg, for whom Harry commenced servant's duties on 13 March.

Mar 16
Lovely day. Went to the baths. In YM in afternoon.

Mar 17
Fine day. Lt Wigg going on leave. Went with him in Staff car to Albert. Fine run. In YMCA in afternoon.

Mar 18
Lovely day. Pictures in afternoon. Very good.

Mar 19
Back at Battery. Worse luck. Raining. On lines again. Put as centre driver.

Mar 20
Raining till noon. Writing.

Mar 21
Misty morning. Piquet. No mail. Bombing. Up with ammunition, at 5.00 am. German advance commenced. They took Doignes and Demicourt. Our guns taken. Major Alexander killed. Captain and several men missing. Went up line with gun team to try to get guns. Awful time! Shelling roads and tracks Machine gun fire in Beaumetz. Couldn't get through. Had to come back to Fremincourt. Several horses and men wounded. Shells creeping ever nearer wagon line.

Mar 22
Lovely weather but misty, No mail. Up line at 5.00 am. Turned back. "Standing to" all day. Guns knocked out retreat began. Left Fremincourt and arrived Bearcourt then on to La Barque at 4.45 am. Out all night in field. Complete mix up of troops.

Mar 23
Very hot. Germans in Beaugay and nearing Fremincourt. The old YM etc blown up. Reveille 8.00 am. Parade 9.00 am. ½ day off. Germans checked. No mail. Bombing near. Slept under a wagon.

Mar 24

At La Barque. Lovely day. Mail arrived. Reveille 6.00 am. Parade 6.30 am. Germans advancing on our right Hermes, Harlincourt, Bus, Ytres. Left La Barque 2.00 pm to Warlincourt. Left again for Le Sars arrived Miramont 3.00 am.

Mar 25

Lovely day. Arrived Miramont. Left again at 6.00 am for Boavry and then on to Mailly-Mailly. Stayed (here in 1916) in Mailly Road for night.

Mar 26

Arrived Mailly-Mailly, Then on to Colincamps.

Mar 27

Lovely day. Left Colincamps for Authie, then on to St Leger for Bienvillers, Sonastro au Bois etc. Pitiful sights here to see the civilians leaving their homes.

Mar 28

Cold but fine. Reveille 7.30 am. Parade at 9.00 am. Arrived at Sardi at 8.00 pm. Heavy rain. Wet through. In a barn. Did about 30k "trek" from Bienvillers Doullens, St Leger etc.

Mar 29

Met Charlie Spencer near Doullens. Also Lt Mor of Pals. Reveille 6.30 am. Moved off at 8.30 am from Sowich, to Wail, near Headin. Lovely village. In barn. No mail to come or to be sent.

Mar 30

Still in Wail. Rain in afternoon. In lines cleaning harness. Rot silly rot. "Dung". Parade at 1.30 pm. Rot again. The British Army commanders not right in their heads. Had some bread given and cigs from Bob from DHR. Heavy rain at night.

Mar 31

Changeable some sun. Reveille 6.30 am and another silly "dung" parade at 9.00 am. Grooming and packing. Moved off from Wail at

1.30 pm. Arrived at Henlin le Sec, near St Pol at 4.00 pm. Then of all things were put on grooming until after 5.00 pm.

APRIL

April 1

Lovely day. Reveille 3.00 am. Move off at 6.30 am. via St Pol and Houdain and Bruay to Hallincourt. Arrived at 2.00 pm. Just like the English mining villages. Stables and a good billet. Brother Wilfred died.

Apr 2

Decent day. Still at Hallincourt. Usual morning parade etc. 2.00 pm exercise order round Barlin etc. Fine. Letters arrive. Saw the first cock fight of my life. Such excitement.

Apr 3

Decent morning. 6.30 am Stables. 9.00 am parade. Exercise in afternoon. Raining a little. Went to Brivary and Lebusiere. Went into 1st Army Headquarters canteen. Supposed to be the best in France. Paid 10F.

Apr 4

Reveille 3.00 am. Raining. Left Hallincourt at 6.30 am. Arrived at Amettes again at 11.00 am. Cleared up. 2.30pm had walk round village.

Apr 5

Rain in morning. Paid 10F at 2.00 pm. Went to Y M at night at Ferfay. Fine place.

Apr 6

Rain at night. Exercise order at 2.00 pm. Y M pictures at night.

Apr 7

Drill etc. No passes given to Lillers. Stayed in at night.

Apr 8

Changeable. Went to Ferfay Y M at night. Mr. Wigg back again. Went across to see him at mess. Came back at 12.00 pm. Starting with him again after making all arrangements with Major Jack.

Apr 9
Dull but fine. Up at 6.30 pm. Left Amettes 2.00 pm. In action at ------? Up all night riding with Mr. Wigg. French houses being looted by our fellows. I billeted in a house with officers.

Apr 10
Nice morning. Up at guns with horses. Some place. Slept in a cart.

Apr 11
Nice day. Awake early. Battery harnessed up. Enemy very close. Returned further back. Machine gun bullets whizzing near by. Returned back again to La Bassee Canal bank.

Apr 12
Nice day. Slept with my horses in a barn. Awoke and found that the battery were galloping along bank side to get across canal. Enemy in field near by. Saddled up and galloped along canal bank in full view of enemy, with Sgt Mjr coming on behind me. My horse stopped on account of dead horse lying on bank side. My horse killed and I thrown off, I don't know how. Luckily I crawled and got safely over the bridge under fire. Arrived at Boanes 11.30 pm . In barn.

Apr 13
At Boanes. Decent house. In mess.

Apr 14
At Boanes. Attack at 6.50 pm. Battery to move in sections. Down at wagon line. Went to DHQ at Malengham with Mr. Wigg. Found that my horse "Jock" was shot in neck. I lost my rubber boots, trumpet etc and music.

Apr 15
At DHQ at Molingham. In church. Playing organ for a time. Shelling Aire. People cleared out of Lillers.

Apr 16
Raining a little. Had a walk round village.

Apr 17
On mess duty. Listening to Rifle Brigade Band. Played "Maid of the Mountains" very well.

Apr 18
In village. Raining. Mr. Wigg put on the Staff.

Apr 19
Round village. Visited house with washing.

Apr 20
Fine day. Went to Aire in afternoon. Buying a few things. Arrived back about 7.0 pm. Had a good time. Heard that J Aird and Roy Goater had been killed. Buried in Lillers cemetery. Same team as self.

Apr 21
Fine day. On mess duty.

Apr 22
Fine day. Parade at 9.00 am. Bombardment 3.00 am until 6.00 am. Went to Aire on cycle. Went to same house as usual for tea. Good time. Arrived back at 6.30pm.

Apr 23
Dull day. Attack by us. Playing football at night v KRR. We won 2.1. Met Sgt in R Bucks who was a Cpl in Con Camp at Boulogne.

Apr 24
Dull morning. Paid 30F

Apr 25
Dull morning. On mess duty.

Apr 26
Decent day. Went to Aire. Shopping. Usual place for tea.

Apr 27
Fine day. Went to Ham in morning. Aire and usual place in afternoon. Bought some chevrons.

Apr 28
Rain at intervals. KRR leaving. Brigadier General Oldfield wounded also Edwards the chaffeur.

Apr 29
Rain at intervals. On mess duty. Went to Aire shopping.

Apr 30
Decent day. In Aire in morning with cook's cart. Round village in afternoon. Shelling at night.

MAY

May 1
Dull but fine. Usual in afternoon.

May 2
Nice and warm. On mess duty. Busy all day.

May 3
Glorious hot day. Leaving Molinghem for Lambres at 10.00 am. Arrived Lambres before 12.00 am. Fine billet for officers. Very nice people here. Piano etc. Played pipe organ in church.

May 4
Went to Molinghem for my watch. Saw several people. Played piano at night at RHMC. Good one.

May 5
Raining heavily. Went to Aire in afternoon. Usual place for tea. Met Lt Harrison going back to Battery. Stayed in Aire until 9.00 pm.

May 6
Went round Tannery at Lambres. Went to Aire again in aft for Mess. Heard organ in cathedral. Foot blown.

May 7
Raining in morn. Heavy bombardment on. Went to Aire in morn. Usual at night. Writing.

May 8
Aire in morning for cigs. Aire at night to theatre. "Blackthorns" 16th Div. Very fine show. Lovely night.

May 9
Ideal day. Aire in morning with cook's cart again. Afternoon reading, writing etc. In garden. Usual at night. In estaminet.

May 10
Dull but fine. Went to Molingham at night. Decent time. Arrived back at 9.30 pm. Playing piano in Mme. Lariaunt's in afternoon.

May 11
Lovely day. Washing and cleaning room etc. Usual at night.

May 12 Very cold and dull. As usual at night.

May 13
Raining. On cycle to Molingham. There catch lorry. Went St Omer for Mess things. Fine town. Visited both etc. Plenty of WRAC's here and lady ambulance drivers. Left 6.30 pm. Arrived Molingham at 8.15 pm. No mail. Cycled back to Lambres and got wet.

May 14
Fine sunny day. Writing all afternoon. Jerry over at night. No mail.

May 15
Lovely day. Writing and reading. Paid out 50F. Jerry over at night.

May 16
Lovely and hot. In Aire in afternoon and night. Usual. Good time. "Plane" bombing very near. Several killed and wounded.

May 17
Hot. Lovely. Cleaning billet etc. First time real drunk at night on Vin Blanc. Felt rotten. Sick etc.

May 18
Lovely day. Bombs smashed Aire up "some".

May 19
Lovely day. On Mess duty. Had Gramophone at billet from Madam. Playing piano etc.

May 20
Lovely day. Moved at 10.00 am from Lambres. to Allouagne, near Lillars. In chateau. Top room. Very decent.

May 21
Lovely day. Went round village.

May 22
Lovely day in open. Playing about at night as usual.

May 23
Lovely day. Went to Auchel in morning by motor. Reading etc. afterward.

May 24
Raining. Left chateau for No 222. Decent place. Billets in 223. Very nice.

May 25
As usual. On Mess duty.

May 26
Lovely day. Went to St Omer for Mess goods in lorry. Back at 5.00 pm. Planes made terrible mess of dump at Arques.

May 27
Lovely day. Heard Band at night. Jerry over.

May 28
Lovely day. Went to see concert party, "Don Acs" at night. Very good.

May 29
Started a servants Mess near officers'. mess. In theatre playing piano. On Mess duty. Paid 50F.

May 30
Nice day. As usual. Met a West Riding fellow in R G A.
Playing piano in afternoon.

May 31
Nice day playing piano in morning and afternoon. Writing after.

JUNE

June 1
Fine day. On Mess duty.

Jun 2
Fine Day. Procession round village of girls going to Mass. Fine. Arthur Gardner in village. Went to hear "Don Acs" at night.

Jun 3
Nice day. At office for being absent from parade. Playing piano in afternoon. Writing after.

Jun 4
Fine but dull. On Mess duty. Lolling round to see people.

Jun 5

Leaving Alloagne at 9.00 am in lorry. Hot day. Arrived at Camblain l'Abbe 2.00 pm, near Aubigny. In hut Mr Wigg and self.
Army Corps Staff here. Very smart. Went to Corps theatre to see "Thistletops"...

Jun 6

Fine day. Paid Battery a visit at Estrie Cauchy. Good time writing later.

Jun 7

Fine day. On Mess duty. No officers to dinner. Had photo taken outside mess.

Jun 8

Fine and hot. Playing cricket part of morning. Writing etc.
Theatre to see "Very Lights" at night. Received photos. A mess.

Jun 9

Rain a little at night. Cycled to Augbigny. Walk at night. Reading and writing. Lots of naughty books to be bought here. Wicked!

Jun 10

Decent day. On mess duty. Awful toothache.

Jun 11

Fine day. Paid 20F. Usual.

Jun 12

Fine day. Played piano in morning. Theatre at night, to see 1st Army Corp "Brass Hats" or the "Rouge at Void". Excellent.

Jun 13

Fine Day. On Mess duty. Mr Wigg in bed. Taking down his meals.

Jun 14

Fine day. Went to Aubigny in afternoon.

Jun 15
Fine day. "Red Drammonds" at theatre. They got the "bird" and not half. Rotten show.

Jun 16
Fine day. On Mess duty. Lots of French people having photos taken.

Jun 17
Fine day. Cycled around. Writing. Theatre at night "Brass Hats". Fine show. Fine girl's dress. Guns in action at Rocklincourt.

Jun 18
Up at 6.30 am. On Mess duty. Moving from Camblain l'Abbe at 10.00 am arrived at Met at 11.30 am. Fine day. No mail. Decent Mess in hut. I have a fine place in Mess for billet.

Jun 19
Raining. Going to Ecurie. What a change at Anzin. Div. Canteen. At Maroul Huts, stables etc there. Trench Fever playing havoc in the camp. No mail.

Jun 20
Fine but rain at night. On Mess duty. No mail. In Y M playing.

Jun 21
Decent day. In Y M in morning. Mail.

Jun 22
Windy and rain. Went to Divisional Canteen. Came back in car. Removed my sleeping from Mess. Whiskey been missing. I know who it is. It is old Gordon, the beggar. Writing.

Jun 23
On Mess duty.

Jun 28
On Mess duty.

June 7, had photo taken outside mess. June 8, received photos. A mess.

Jun 29
Nice day. Walk round village.

Jun 30
Very hot. Went to South Army Hut, near here to a show.

JULY

July 1
Very hot and fine. On Mess duty.

Jul 2
Very hot. In village at Y M playing.

Jul 3
Windy and colder. On fatigues in afternoon. Writing at night. General Oldfield back again.

Jul 4
Cold then lovely. On Mess duty.

Jul 5
Dull. In Y M at morning. Fatigues in afternoon. No mail.

Jul 6
Decent day. In Y M morning. Passed doctor for Commission.

Jul 7
Hot day. On Mess duty. Divisional Band, playing.

Jul 8
Hot day. To Divisional Canteen. B Battery had 25 killed and 16 wounded horses by a 4.2 shell.

Jul 9
Rain then fine. On Mess duty. went up line with Mr Wigg in motor as far as ridge in front of Rocklincourt to try new time lights for signals.

Jul 10
Heavy rain at night then a glorious sky.

Jul 11
Rain at intervals. On Mess duty. Y M at morning. Writing.

Jul 12
Rain at morning. Jerry over.

Jul 13
Fine and warm. On mess duty. In village.

Jul 14
Fine day. Canadians coming in. Left Mareruil at 9.30 am. Arrived at Bajus, near Houdan, 2 .00 pm. Lorry part way. Heavy rain. In chateau. Bed at 12.00 am. Very nice people here.

Jul 15
Reveille 4.00 am. Breakfast 5.30 am. Leave Bajus 6.30 am. Entrain at Pernes at 12 am. Passed Abbeville, Etaples etc.

Jul 16
Fine and very hot. Passed through Eu, saw Paris, St Germain and Versailles. Canteen girls threw favours and gave us wine and coffee on platform. Saw Palace of Versailles quite closely. Arrived at Pont sur Seine at 3 pm. Beautiful country and villages. "Trek" of 15 k to Font St Denis.

Jul 17
Fine and very hot. At Font St Denis. Fine Billets. On Mess duty. Nice people. People giving wines when on '"trek" and favours. German attack north of here, near Havre. Terrible storm and hurricane at night. Up all night.

Jul 18
Fine day. Left Fontain St Denis at 5.15 am with transport. Germans attacking. Stop at Marain Pierre. Nice place.

Jul 19
Very hot day. Left Marain Pierre at 9.30 am, via Sonberres and arrived at Hautvillers, near Epernay. Big place and lovely chateaux. Stayed night. German plane struck dump and station at Epernay. Some sight. French attack at Soisssons 10,000 Prisoners 200 Guns. Germans near Marne.

Jul 20
Left Hautvillers for St Imoges.

Jul 21
At St Imoges. Hot day. On mess duty.

Jul 22
Hot day. Went a ride on horse.

Jul 23
Raining. On Mess duty. Boys over the top again. Heavy rain. Left St Imoges 5.00 pm for Hautevilles 7.00 pm again. Cleared up. In chateau. Beautiful place.

Jul 24
Lovely day. Went in motor lorry to Seganny for Mess goods. Some place. About 40 k there. Ill at night. Fumes of petrol I think.

Jul 25
On Mess duty. Had a glorious lunch. Stewed meat, potatoes, bread, cold meat, tomatoes, onions and salad, tapioca pudd and tea. Some feed.

Jul 26
Raining part of day. Went a motor ride to Hansey, then up the line to Nanteul. Playing piano at night. Washing clothes etc.

Jul 27
Raining to 5.00 pm. On Mess duty. Left Hautevillers after tea to Nanteul Headquarters. Journey of about 8 k.

Jul 28
Decent day. Still at Nanteul. Funny place and very weird.

Jul 29
Fine day. On Mess duty. Went up to Battery. Sgt Hendry killed.

Jul 30
Fine day. Going up to Infantry Headquarters with Mr Wigg at Chamongy, for 2 nights. Got a gas alarm when in bed but nothing came of it. Dodging a few high bursts.

Jul 31
Fine clear day. At Brigade Headquarters Chamongy. Rum ration. Shelling in village all afternoon. Left Chamongy at 11.30 pm. Heavy shelling of roads. Ducking down into trenches at roadside. Smell of gas. Motor met us half way back.

AUGUST

Aug 1
Left Nanteul at 1.00 pm, for entraining at Epernay. Went in big champagne factories and of course brought heaps of bottles back to train. Left Epernay at 7.00 pm.

Aug 2
Raining most of day. Passed through Amiens. Knocked about. On Mess duty on train. Some job.

Aug 3
Decent day. Arrived at Pernes at 5.00 am again. In chateau. Fine place. Lorry then to Aubigny again. In big chateau there. Fine place. 4 years of it.

Aug 4
Arrived Aubigny, 11.00 am. Lovely day. In village I know so well. Playing football at night. Washing up etc.

Aug 5
Dull day. On Mess duty. Permission to play on piano at 5.00 pm. Writing.

Aug 6
Raining. Leaving Aubigny for Viller-Chattel other side of Aubigny. Mr. Wigg temporary G.S.O.Z. Playing piano in morn. Lot of work. Finished at 11.00 pm.

Aug 7
Rotten place. Viller-Chattel. Nothing much to do. Divisional Commander here. Went to Aubigny on cycle at night.

Aug 8
Fine day. Went to Aubigny and then on to Acq. Saw the King pass in motor. We formed guard of honour on road. Commission papers arrived. Had them signed by General.

Aug 9
Nice day. Mr Wigg seeing about comm. Went to Aubigny for pay.

Aug 10
Nice day. Went to Hirgoval.

Aug 11
Nice day. Going to Acq for signatures of Colonel, doctor for Comm papers. Call at Augbigny. Got sigs. Walked from Acq to Augbigny, then cycle.

Aug 12
Nice day. Hot. Went to Augbigny in morning. Stayed to lunch and tea. Went to Hirgoval at night.

Aug 13
Nice and hot. Went to Camblain Neul and Camblain l'Abbe. No 13 Estaminet "out of bounds" and no wonder. Saw a cricket match at Corps Camp. Pedlar, the South African playing, also the 8th and 20th

Divisional Bands. Fine affair. Then to Augbigny and walked from there to Viller-Chattel.

Aug 14
Nice day. Writing in morning. At Augbigny afterward.

Aug 15
At Augbigny. Stayed late.

Aug 16
Leaving Viller-Chattel for Mareouil again. In action.
Arrived at Maroeuil 12.00 pm. Down road at No 2 hut.
We slept in a dug out by the Artillery Mess.

Aug 17
Dull and hot. Up at 5.00 am. Looking after another officer, Major Fergus RS. In YM in afternoon. Playing piano.

Aug 18
Very hot day. Up at usual time. In Y M at morn. Writing.

Aug 19
Fine day. In Y M at morn. Went to a "A" Battery 311 Brigade at night. Met QMS Glascodine. Lying at Mont St Elvi. Long talk.

Aug 20
Fine day. In Y M at morn. Writing in afternoon. Baths. Out for a short time in village at night.

Aug 21
Very hot. Jerry bombing and shelling. Bombing near huts. Lump of shrapnel pierced Mr Wigg's hut tearing his burberry.

Aug 22
Fine and hot. Went to Aubigny. Good time. Stayed in Maroeuil.

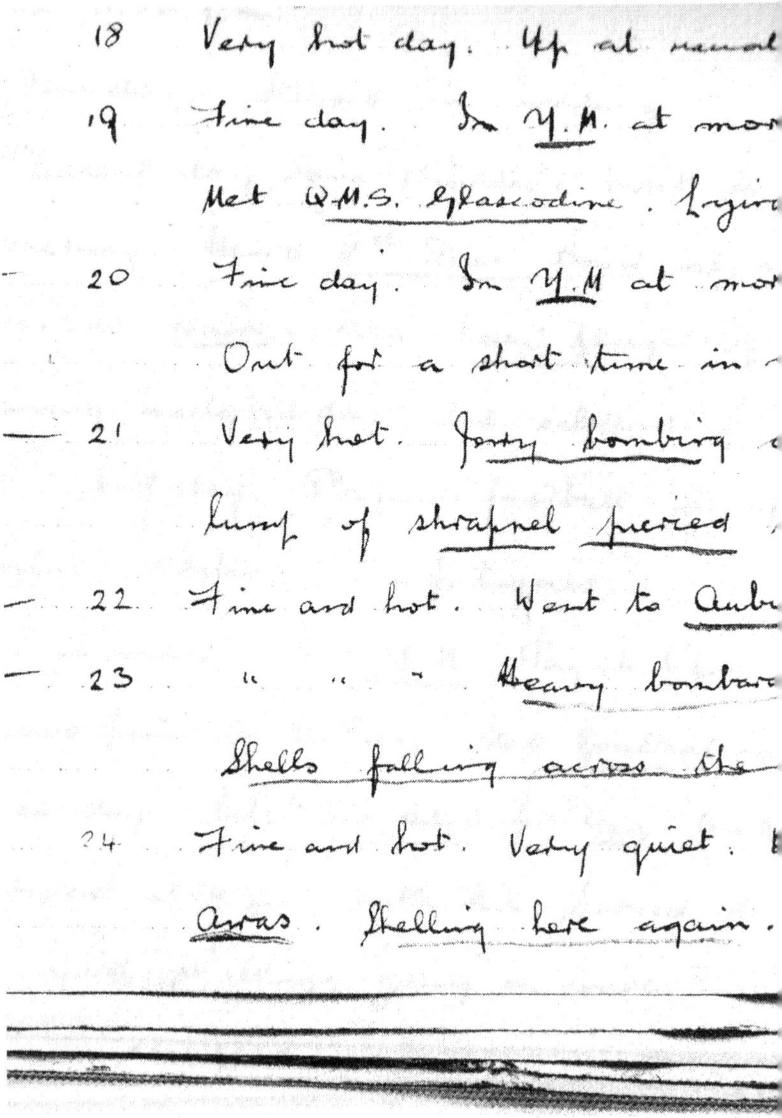

18 Very hot day. Up at usual

19 Fine day. In Y.M. at mor

Met Q.M.S. Glascodine. Lyin

— 20 Fine day. In Y.M at mor

Out for a short time in

— 21 Very hot. Jerry bombing

lump of shrapnel pierced

— 22 Fine and hot. Went to Aub

— 23 " " " Heavy bombar

Shells falling across the

24 Fine and hot. Very quiet.

Arras. Shelling here again.

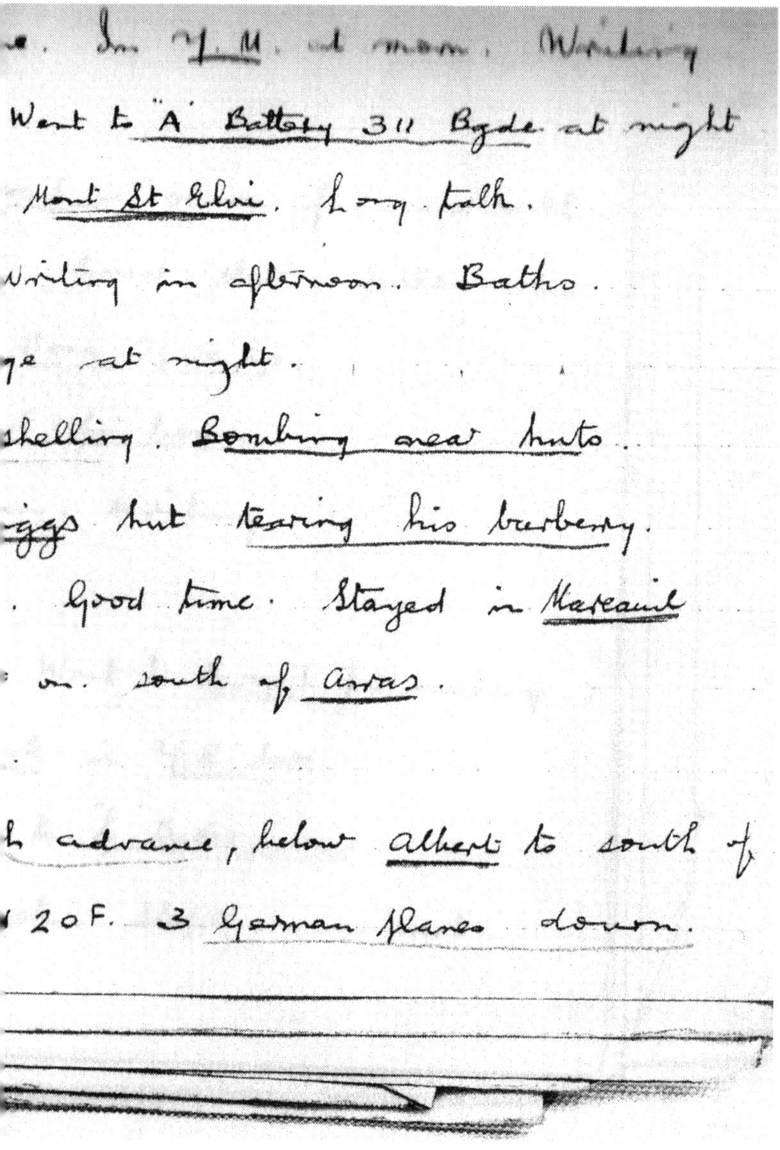

e. In Y.M. at morn. Writing

Went to "A" Battery 311 Bgde at night

Mont St Eloi. Long talk.

Writing in afternoon. Baths.

ge at night.

shelling. Bombing near huts.

iggs hut tearing his burberry.

. Good time. Stayed in Mareuil

on. south of Arras.

.

h advance, below Albert to south of

1 20F. 3 German planes down.

Aug 23
Fine and hot. Heavy bombardment on south of Arras. Shells falling across the road.

Aug 24
Fine and hot. Very quiet. British advance, below Albert to south of Arras. Shelling here again. Paid 20 F. 3 German planes down.

Aug 25
Nice day. Went to Acq. and Augbigny. Dinner at Acq. Good day.

Aug 26
Rained a little. We took Monedy and Baupaume again. Moved from Maroeuil to Larient-Blangy, near Arras. Decent billets, but my dug out with lots of rats.

Aug 27
Dull day. Planes busy in morn. In Arras. Cycled. Looks much different.

Aug 28
Raining almost all day. Writing to have interview for Comm at Augbigny on 5th.

Aug 29
Fine day. Prisoners coming down. Arras in afternoon. Writing.

Aug 30
Fine day. Left Larient-Blangy for Victory Camp, Rocklincourt. Sleeping in huts. Dug out here 60 steps deep.

Aug 31
Fine day. Went to Maroeuil in afternoon for washing.

SPETEMBER

Sept 1
Decent day. Went to hear "Balmorals" at night in "Turnip Tops". Very fine show.

Sep 2
Rather cold and windy.

Sep 3
Nice day. On fatigues in morning. Went to Y M Divisional Band playing. Went to Maroeuil at night, also to see 311 Brigade. Met Severs in Sgt's Mess. Good time. Back at 9.00 pm.

Sep 4
Nice day. On fatiques at 2.30 pm. Writing etc.

Sep 5
Nice day. Went to Augbigny for test in RAF. Get Mr Wigg 2 stars, health salts, matches, sponge etc. Called at Acq to see 49th Divisional Artillery. Met Norman Drake. Walked back from Acq to camp at 11.30 pm.

Sep 6
Fine day. Stayed in writing.

Sep 7
Decent day, some thunder. Went to Maroeuil in morn for and with washing. Heard 8th Divisional Band at night. Good. Met a fellow who was at Havre. Also horn player of Carl Rosa Opera Co.

Sep 8
Raining nearly all day. Not selected by RAF for Comm.

Sep 9
Raining part day. Playing football in afternoon. Writing.

Sep 10
Rain. Writing. On fatigues.

Sep 11
Rain in morn. In Y M. Pay at 6.00 pm. 30 f. Went to Maroeuil for washing.

Sep 12
Heavy rain. W's birthday. Met Gummersal and Jack in Y M here.

Sep 13
Nice day. Left Divisional Headquarters for Acq, back now to "C" Battery 255. Arrived at 4.00 pm with kit. Served dinner etc. Slept in a cart in yard. Mr. Wigg going on leave.

Sep 14
Sent on lines for duty until Mr. Wigg comes back. Rotten. Doing odd jobs such as cleaning lines etc. Moved billet to a barn with the crowd. Very damp. What a change. Went to Maroeuil at night.

Sep 15
Nice day. Went to Augbigny in afternoon. Decent time. Had tea there. Jerry bombing there.

Sep 16
Fine and hot. On lines. Had supper at Mess. Went to hear Balmorals at night. Good. Awful thunderstorm at night.

Sep 17
Hot and fine. On lines. Stayed in village at night.

Sep 18
Nice day. Helping the fitter. Gas drill in morning. Writing at night.

Sep 19
Nice day. On lines.

Sep 20
Rain in morn. Writing at night.

Sep 21
Heavy rain in morn. Paid out at 2.00 pm. 15 F. Had a good time in village. Heaps of fellows dead drunk but not this child.

Sep 22
Rain in afternoon. Orders to move 3.30 pm, then cancelled. Parade 2.00 pm. Harness up, Major back again.

Sep 23
Rain part day. Still at Acq. In village at night round a few old spots.

Sep 24
Lovely day. German plane dropping "Peace" pamphlets. Left Acq at 3.30 pm for Madagascar Stables arrived at 6.00 pm. Rode a horse singly there. Parade at 7.30 pm. Jerry over again about 8.00 pm.

Sep 25
Rain in morn, fine in aft. Major goes on leave. Playing football at night. Jerry over in heaps.

Sep 26
Nice day. Exercise order before breakfast. Finished on lines. Writing.

Sep 27
In Mess again, thank goodness. Nice day. Down at Maroeuil with washing. Wagon lines moved to St Nicholas. In broken down house for Mess.

Sep 28
Changeable day. Making a new store in Mess.

Sep 29
Fine but cold. Writing. Heavy rain at night. Rumours of Bulgar surrender. British almost at Cambrai and outflanking Douai. Belge advance. Taken Dixminde, Paschandale and Messines Ridge.

Sep 30
Decent in morn, heavy rain at night. W. Wigg back again. Good. More victories.

OCTOBER

Oct 1

Nice day. 5 gone on leave. Rode on horse to Maroeuil for washing. Going up to guns in afternoon. Went up with mess cart. Slept with F sub in iron place. Lots of rats.

Oct 2

Decent day. Forward guns coming out at 6.00 pm. Rear position firing from 8.30 to 9.30 pm.

Oct 3

Rear position coming out at 2.30 pm . Arrived at Harbarcq. Decent place. Arrived at 7.00 pm.

Oct 4

Nice day. Paid out 15 F. Had photos taken in group. All the servants. Playing piano in Mess afterwards.

Oct 5

Dull day. Leaving Harbarcq at 10.15 am. Stayed for rest at the Larient Bridges for a few hours, then moved down the Arras – Cambrai Road at dark to Cagincourt. Arrived 10.00 pm. Slept in very little funk holes. Awful!

Oct 6

Dull and drizzle. Left Cagincourt for action at 2.00 pm. Arrived outside Raillescourt, 5 k from Cambrai. In open.

Oct 7

Rain part of day. Digging ourselves in all day. Bourlon Wood on our right.

Oct 8

Nice morning. Heavy bombardment in morning. Finished digging. 5 of us slept in cookhouse. Cambrai and Douai burning.

The Church at Bourlon, by William Rothenstein.

Oct 9

Nice day. Bombing in morning. Advance on our right. Our guns supporting Canadians. Cambrai taken. Jerry can't be found, he's on the run. Seen 4 or 5 K forward.

Oct 10

Decent but dull. Wagon lines come up to edge of famous Bourlon Wood. Memories.

Oct 11

Moved Mess to house in Raillincourt. Decent night spent. Tons of traffic going forward through Cambrai. Moved again. Slept on a railway embankment under a sheet. Raining. Very dark. Tommy Hayes thrown from wagon and hurt.

Oct 12

Dull day. My birthday. What a day for a birthday. No time to think about it. Moved forward again in front of Cambrai. 49th, 51st, 4th, 39th Divisions here. Barrage at 12 noon. Open warfare. Barrage on Lieu Hermin. Slight south of Valenciennes.

Oct 13

A wicked day. Barrage fired at 9.00 am. Terrible shell fire from enemy at same time. Mr Wigg killed in front of guns near front line and windmill. Helped to find him and carry him back. Terribly smashed up. Shell fire hellish. We moved back at night to wagon line at Irvy. Avences le Sec. I was about last to go back. Men blown up and horses. Awful sights here. Heaps killed. Slept under a wagon. Infantry come back to old position of night before.

Oct 14

Bright day. Still heavy shelling. At wagon line. Mr Wigg's body going down to DAC. Took over two big horses to drive officer's wagon.

Oct 15

Mr. Capt Wigg's funeral, DAC provided a GS wagon for the body. I was one of the bearers to graveside. A party of us went on horses from

Battery. Buried near Ramillies Station, near Cambrai. Wagon line moved to Cambrai Road. Slept under wagon.

Oct 16
Raining all morning. In "bivvy" with "F" sub.

Oct 17
Dull day. As usual. Piquet at night. 2nd turn.

Oct 18
Fog in morn. Cold. Harness cleaning in morning. Rot.

Oct 19
Dull day. Up line in afternoon with rations, kit etc. to Ivry and over to Avensnes le Sec. 2 journeys. Awful. Back to Escauduennes at night.

Oct 20
Raining. Advance. Moved from Escauduennes to Irvy in morning. Up line again to Avensnes le Sec and to guns in afternoon and back to Irvy at night. 4 go on leave.

Oct 21
Raining. Left Irvy at 5.00 am for Avensnes le Sec. Guns advanced again. Left Avensnes le Sec for Noyelles in afternoon near Denrain, a large place. Wagon lines in open. Civilians here.

Oct 22
Raining in morning. Left Noyelles. Sleeping in Mess. Decent place. Shelling near the house.

Oct 23
Fine day. Moved into stable then out to lines again. In "bivvy" at night. Guns go forward at 4.15pm

Oct 24
Dull morning. 6 hours Bombardment on. Prisoners coming down and 6 German officers. Left Noyelles for Thiant. In big store. Jerry shelling close by and breaking glass on roof. Slept in factory.

Oct 25
Decent day. Shelling. Advance of 2,000 yards.

Oct 26
Fine day. 10 going on leave. Advance again. Heavy shelling on roads. Lots of civilians and Germans coming down. Australian Calvary here. Lots of horses killed on road.

Oct 27
Fine day. Civilians in yard. Mostly women.

Oct 28
As usual. Playing piano in Sgt's mess. Down a dug out at night. 2 drivers wounded in B sub. 3 horses killed.

Oct 29
Went to Lieu St Armand for ordnance stores. Left Thiant for Moncheaux to wagon lines. In barn for a billet. In Mess playing.

Oct 30
Fine day. In Thiant in afternoon for straw. In Mess playing.

Oct 31
Raining. In village for straw. Mess playing at night.

NOVEMBER

Nov 1
Decent day. Big stunt. Heavy Barrage. Advance. Prisoners. Out for canteen things. Went to Villers et Lauchy, Lieu St Armand, Douchy, Halchain, Thiant, Moncheaux.

Nov 2
Raining a little. Prisoners in again. Hundreds. In mess at night. Word of leave through. Hurrah!

Nov 3
Dull day. Moving wagon lines in morn to Maing. Arrived at Maing in

afternoon. Guns going forward at night. Teams up. "Jocks" made a big bayonet charge here. 70 forward position at 5.00 am.

Nov 4
Rain at night. Fine stables and billets here. Lots of pianos. 3 going on leave. I among 10 more going on leave. Cheers. Left Maing at 1.30 pm walked to Douchy and caught a lorry to Cambrai, then caught ammunition train to Brisleau and caught up with leave train to Arras with men whose leave commenced on the 6th. Raining at night.

Nov 5
At Arras. Left at 11.30 am. Went to YM. Changed to Calais train at Arras Arrived in Calais at 9.30 pm. Went to No. 6 Rest Camp. Had supper.

Nov 6
Raining. Left Calais 12.15 pm. Boat left at 2.00 pm. Arrived Dover 3.30 pm. Arrived London at 6.30 pm Stayed the night at Catholic Club. Lovely place. Sent telegrams and bought clothes.

Nov 7
Caught 8.50 am from St Pancras. Arrived Bradford 2.45 pm. No one to meet me. Fancy.

Nov 8
Raining. ON LEAVE.

Nov 11
Armistice signed. Fine. All guns etc. cease at 11.00 am.

Nov 20
Leave finishes. Left Bradford at 8.55 pm. Midland. W saw me off. Rotten going back when all is over. Arrived Leeds at 9.30 pm.

Nov 21
Arrived London 5.00 am. Stayed London for a day. Went to Oxford to see "Better Ole" and Carlton Pic House at night.

Nov 22
Caught train to Dover and saw load of 1st British prisoners arrive. Sirens hooters and bands playing. Arrived Calais before tea. Concert at night at YM. Stayed in Camp night.

Nov 23
Left Calais 5.00 am. Passed Douai and got out at Bouchain. Then motor lorry to Valenciennes. Met Bob Severs. Then to Douchy then lorry to Mons. Stayed there the night in station.

Nov 25
Left Mons at 9.30 am and arrived at Givry to Battery at dinnertime. Went in village to see "Follies" Good.

Nov 26
Parade at 9.00 am on lines. As usual. Long hours. Paid at 2.00 pm. Took over temp groom to QMS. and sub Sgt. Rotten food. In bed early.

Nov 27
Dull day. On exercise. Rotten dinner. Parade 1.45 pm. Letters.

Nov 28
Raining. Moved off at morning to Roeulx. Arrived at 4.00 pm. Stables in barns and factory. Fine. Billets very poor and cramped. Heavy rain.

Nov 29
Still Sgt's groom. Parades as usual. Inoculated in afternoon. 2 days off. Went to Prince de Groys chateau to Divisional Headquarters to see some of the boys. Fine place.

Nov 30
Fine day but cold. Went up to chateau after staying in bed all morning.

DECEMBER

Dec 1
Dance at chateau at 8.00 pm also one in village.

Dec 2
Playing piano in Sgt's Mess at night.

Dec 3
Went to chateau in afternoon to commence Mess duty once more for 255 Brigade. Fine place.

Dec 4
At chateau. Playing at Sgt's mess in afternoon.

Dec 5
Fine day. Lovely dinner. Guest night. 28 officers to dinner.

Dec 6
Fine day. At Sgt's Mess.

Dec 7
Went to play organ at Roeulx church with organist. Not so bad.

Dec 8
Lovely day. Full dinner at mid-day. Big dance at school. Light dinner at 7.30 pm. Night off for me. Removing my billet from chateau to a new one in village.

Dec 9
At new billet 26 Petit Rue. Nice people.

Dec 10
Raining.

Dec 11
Raining. Sent back to Battery at 9.00 am. On fatiques in morning. Whitewashing etc. ½ day off but I was put on harness cleaning in afternoon. The dirty dogs.

Dec 12
Usual.

Dec 13
Concert in the Town Hall at 3.00 pm. Went there.

Dec 14
Raining. Working on harness in afternoon. Concert at night. Sang "Perfect Day".

Dec 15
Fine day. At church in morning. Football in afternoon. We lost 7.0. On piquet at night.

Dec 16
Raining. Slept at chateau at night.

Dec 17
Dull day. Usual. Writing.

Dec 18
Raining at night. Playing in church in afternoon.

Dec 19
Playing with Officers Rugger Team "C" Battery in afternoon. We won 11.0. Rugby Union.

Dec 20
Commenced servant to Capt. Smail at 4 Rue des Tournais. Playing at Cinema at night. Once again a change.

Dec 21
Rain at night. No show.

Dec 22
Rain at night. Playing cinema at night. Full house. Writing.

Dec 23
Raining. Not playing at Cinema.

Dec 24
Fine morning. Frosty. First fall of snow. Playing at "D" Battery Dance at night at Grand Place. Good night.

Dec 25
Snow. Lovely day. Dinner at 12.30 pm. Playing for concert at "D" Battery. Dancing afterward. Fine. Finished at 11.00 pm. Went to football match in afternoon. "D" 1 Headquarters 1.

Dec 26
Lovely day. Cold. No mail. Mr Smail going away for day. Madame giving the boys in billet a feed at night. 8.30 pm. Had a good time. Went to La Louvierre in afternoon.

Dec 27
Raining. Gyms in morning. Writing.

Dec 28
Heavy rain. Cinema at night.

Dec 29
Raining in morn.

Dec 30
In Mons at morning, shopping with Capt Smail. Went in motor. Came back with Mess Cart. In at night.

Dec 31
Nice day. Played Rugger in afternoon 6.6. Invitation to "D" Battery Dance at 6.45 pm. Had dinner at Battery. Played for concert and dance. Back home 1.00 am.

1919

JANUARY

Jan 1

Nice day. Washing in morning. Watching football match in afternoon. Stayed in at night writing. Had supper at 4 Rue des Tous.

Jan 2

Decent day. Took shoes to mend and ironed slacks.

Jan 3

Nice day. Busy day. Big Officers' Ball at Chateau. Cutting bread for sandwiches etc. Running around with orders. Serving at dinner. English and Belgian ladies to dinner. Lovely. Got home at 1.00 am.

Jan 4

Review by Corp Comm of Artillery in Roeulx. Fine show.

Jan 5

Usual day. Church etc.

Jan 6

Playing in house with the old man "Tiddly winks". Beat him every game at 19 Grand Rue. Cinema at night. Then to supper at No 4.

Jan 7

Nice day. Playing organ in morn. Afternoon as usual. Writing at night. Put notice up re musical theory lessons for men of Battery.

Jan 8

½ day off and usual.

Jan 9
Usual. Dancing in estaminet a little.

Jan 10
Playing at Officers' NCO Dance of "D" Battery at Grand Place. Finish at 11.00 pm. Good time.

Jan 11
Dull and rain. Rugby match Artillery v Seaforths.11.3. Village at night.

Jan 12
Dancing and playing at "A" Battery in school. Good. No mail.

Jan 13
Usual day. No mail. In village at night.

Jan 14
No mail. at night. Writing.

Jan 15
Raining. Ball of "C" Battery in Cafe du Parc. Playing not bad. Rather crowded. Home at 12.15 am.

Jan 16
Lovely day. Usual in morning and afternoon. To chateau for gramophone. Went to "D" battery at night and writing. No mail. A rough house in billet.

Jan 17
Nice day. No mail. Washing and writing in morn. Packing up in afternoon for Capt. Rugger Match Artillery v Royal Scots 0.14. Dancing at "D" Battery at night. Washing clothes. No mail.

Jan 18
Rain at night. On fatigues in afternoon 2.00 pm. Changed billet to 13 Grand Rue. Didn't go to Grand Rue after all. Capt away for night. Bad lad.

Jan 19
Playing for "A" Battery at night. Quite a funny evening. Billet received at 3, Grand Rue then told I couldn't have it at 10pm at night.

Jan 20
Lovely day. Playing wing 3/4 for left section at Rugger. Left section won 9.0. Lt Stokes hurt in the match, good job. Packing up at night etc.

Jan 21
With Capt's kit to Mons in morning. Cold but nice. Good time coming back. Made several calls. Dancing at "D" Battery at night. Supper at billet. Writing.

Jan 22
Fine and cold. "C" Battery Officers' and NCOs Dance at Grand Place. Good affair. I played. Finished at 11.45 pm. No parade all day.

Jan 23
A little snow. Very cold. Commenced servant to Capt Bissett. Soccer match Left v Right Section. Played for left section. Draw 1.1. At chateau at night 8.00 pm. Played during dinner and after for dancing. Heaps to eat and drink. General there. Home at 12.30 am.

Jan 24
Lovely but cold. Changed billet to 3, Place de l'Eglise. Chemists. Fine place. At 28 Petit Rue at 2.00 pm. 4.15 pm at Chateau to play for afternoon dance. English Sisters there. Went to play for dance at DAC Headquarters at Eccaussines. Fine affair. Good time. Back at 4.00 am.

Jan 25
Nice day. As usual. At billet at night. Having some sport.

Jan 26
Snowing heavily. Church at 10.00 am. At billet at night. Madam out good time. Writing after.

Jan 27
Snow. Usual. Snow fight in morning for exercise in football field. Billet at night.

Jan 28
Nice day. Played at dance at Eccaussines at night. No 1 Sect DAC Dance at Cinema. Went by horse and trap. Arrived back 3.30 am. The "Twilight Waltz".

Jan 29
Usual day. Ball at Chateau. Prince of Wales seeing Batteries.

Jan 30
Playing at Chateau at night. Guest night. Finish 3.00 am. Young blind drunk. Had to drag him home. Laugh.

Jan 31
Snow still. Going to dance at "B" Battery. Finish 1.00 am.

FEBRUARY

Feb 1
Fine day. Playing at dance in the La Louvierre in morning.

Feb 2
Usual. Skating on the lake at Chateau. Boil in my neck.

Feb 3
Fine day. Usual.

Feb 4
Snowing. Presentation of medals at Chateau. MM. (One I should have had for Oct 13 stunt).

Feb 5
Heavy snowstorm. No mail. Playing for dance at 8pm at Roeulx. English and Belgium ladies there. Dresses lovely. Finished at 4.00 am. Lovely house and room. Madam Naveau.

255th (Highland) Brigade
R. F. A.

DANCE

Rœulx Château

PRINCE DE CROY

WEDNESDAY 29th JANUARY 1919.

PIANO . H. WESTERMAN

VIOLIN MORRICE, CRAIG
CELLO SIMPSON

Feb 6
Lovely day. RA (W) Band playing 2.30 pm at Cinema. Fine. Playing piano at chateau for dinner. Capt Stanley and General there. No Mail. Finished 12.30 am.

Feb 7
Nice but cold. Boil on neck about better. "D" Batt lost cup to "A" Batt 1.0. Feed at billet at 8.00 pm. No mail.

Feb 8
Frosty. Pictures at night, "The Welsh Singer".

Feb 9
Frosty. Cut my finger but played for service. Moved off. Billet to 7 at M Schmidt Sleeping in an attic bedroom. Fine place. No mail.

Feb 10
Nice day. Usual. Football for ½ an hour in morning. Lecture by Stokes at 2.00 pm. Having a bath afterward. Cinema at night. No mail.

Feb 11
Nice day. Skating in afternoon. Borrowed skates from M Schmidt. Out to tea at Madam Huart, Petit Rue. Dancing at Madam Naveau at night. Nice "do". No mail.

Feb 12
Nice day. Playing and dancing at Madam Naveau. Learnt a new Hesitation Waltz and teaching the steps for new sequence Fox Trots. No mail.

Feb 13
Fine. Skating in afternoon. Good "do". Dance at chateau 8.00 pm. Playing. Fine affair. Home at 4.00 am. At Madam Naveau in afternoon. Still no mail.

Feb 14
Stayed in bed until after 9.00 am. Playing for "B" Battery dance at 8.00 pm. Grand Place. Finish 1.00 am. Decent. At Madam Naveau until 7.30 pm. No mail.

Feb 15
Nice day. Thawing. Playing football with "C" Battery v "A" Battery. We lost 0.1. Ground like a duck pond. Stayed in at night. No mail. About 11th day without mail. Writing about it. Only 9 men going home demob.

Feb 16
Played for church service in morning 10.00 am. Letters arrived at last. Playing for select dance of Battery and Divisional Headquarters. About 27 to 28 couples. Lovely. 10F. 3 violins. 1 cello and piano.

Feb 17
Went to Maurage for coal for Capt in morning. Dancing at Madam Naveau in afternoon. In early at night.

Feb 18
Decent day. Playing football in afternoon. Left v Centre. Playing for Left. We won 5.0. I scored third goal. Commencing servant to little Lt Lorrimer, as well.

Feb 19
Decent day. No mail. At Madam Naveau at night dancing.

Feb 20
Decent day. Feeling rotten and sickly. Played piano at chateau after dinner.

Feb 21
Feeling washed out, and no wonder. Dance at 4.30 pm at Mme Naveau. I to dance and play. English ladies to be there.

Feb 22
Cinema at night. Good picture.

Feb 23
Playing for Headquarters Dance. Finish 1.00 am. Good time.

Feb 24
Nice day. Playing Rugger with left versus right section. We lost 6.8. I scored the six points for Left. Stayed in at night.

Feb 25
Dull day. Playing at dance at Eccausines. DAC No 1 34 Dances. Arrived back at 4.00 am.

Feb 26
Changeable. Playing Rugger in afternoon with Possibles v Probables. We won 16.0. Scored 2 tries. Good game. Chateau at night.

Feb 27
Decent day. Playing at chateau at 10.30 am. Cinema at night.

Feb 28
Playing at chateau at 10.30 am. In Houndheng at night. Heard a couple of fine accordion players in estaminet.

MARCH

Mar 1
Lovely day. Chateau in morning for piano practice. Mme Naveau's at night. Writing after.

Mar 2
Playing for church Service. Playing for Jazz Band at night at chateau. Had heaps of fun. Home 3.30 am.

Mar 3
Raining. Usual.

Mar 4
Playing for a special officers' dance at chateau at Eccaussines. Divisional DAC Dance. Several Generals etc there. Ladies, Counts etc. Fine and really beautiful dance and place. Went by motor lorry. Back at 4.30 am. Some feed.

Mar 5
Nice day. Stayed in bed until 2.30 pm. Cinema at night.

Mar 6
Raining. Usual day.

Mar 7
Cinema at night.

Mar 8
Raining. Usual. Playing piano at Madam Huart, then cinema.

Mar 9
Dance at No 18 Rue des Mons. Headquarters dance. Very good. Good time. Finished 1.00 am.

Mar 10
Changeable day. At 19 Grand Rue in afternoon. Good time. Went with Turner. Playing piano at organist's house at night. Home 11.00 pm.

Mar 11
Nice day. Cinema at night, then to Madame at Rue Des Mons to play piano. Good night.

Mar 12
Music at night. Had photo taken on grey horse of Major's. In garden of Mme Schmidt. Playing football in afternoon with "C" Battery v "B" Battery. We won 9.1. I scored 3 goals. Had a walk at night.

Mar 13
Lovely day. Played piano at Houdberg in morning. Going in trap to play for dance at Central Hotel. Eccaussines at 6.15 pm, No 3 Sec DAC dance. 10 Frc. Had accident coming back. Had 2 girls in trap and shafts broke and threw all into road. "Binkie" badly cut and one of the girls moaning and what not. Had to walk back to Roeulx. Back at 5.30 am. What a night.

Photograph taken 12 March 1919,
in garden of Mme Schmidt.

Mar 14
Lovely day. CInema at night, then to bed early.

Mar 15
Dull day. "Bink" in bed bandaged up. Playing football with "C" v "A" Battery. We lost 2.1. Played right half back. Went to Houdberg at night. Met them. Turner went with one and I caught the tram back.

Mar 16
Played in "Rugger" match with officers, played full back and got "bumped" some. We lost 24.0. General watching. I was complimented on my good play. Went to La Louvierre afterward. Played for dance at 18 Rue de Mons. Good affair. Had a good time.

Mar 17
Nice day. At La Louvierre in afternoon. Dance at Grand Place. Came home at 10.30 pm.

Mar 18
Nice day. Cinema at night. Packing up.

Mar 19
Up at 7.30 am. Capt. Bissett going home. Lucky devil. Played at cinema at night and then played at 256 Brigade concert. Rotten show. 10F.

Mar 20
Playing at chateau and cinema. Finished 12.00 pm.

Mar 21
Went to Brussels with "Bink" 1.10 pm train. Arrived 3.00 pm. Stayed at a hotel outside the Gare du Midi. Madam Picheron. Went roller skating in afternoon. Some afternoon. Went roller skating at night and of course got into the usual dark houses unknowingly. Good time.

Mar 22
Stayed in bed until 11.00 am. Breakfast in the city. Catching the 2.44 pm back. Nice weather.

Mar 23
Back at Roeulx. Playing for "A" Battery dance at 18 Rue des Mons at 7.00 pm. 10F. Finished 1.00 am.

Mar 24
Raining. Moved from Roeulx to Marage by lorry at 11.00 am. Billet for self and officer at No 4 Grand Rue. Mme Dalhoussiere, Chemists. Nice house. Playing piano to charm Mme to give me a room. I did not get one.

Mar 25
Cold day but fine. Playing piano etc.

Mar 26
Turner going to England. In billet by myself. Fine time.

Mar 27
Went to Jolimont at night and La Fourierre in afternoon.

Mar 28
Snowing heavily. Usual. Playing on a lovely piano in estaminet next door. Feeling very ill at night.

Mar 30
Playing for Artillery Headquarters Dance at Grand Place, Roeulx. Slept at Roeulx. Not as good a dance as last one. A lot of pros there from La Loun.

Mar 31
Caught 7.00 am car back to Marage. Crowded. Usual during day.

APRIL

April 1
Nice day. Still a cold and headache. Change of life and living.

Apr 2
Lovely day. Having fun in cafe, Grand Rue.

Apr 3
Lovely day. Playing for dance at 49 Grand Rue, Marage. 10f 7.00 pm. Good time. Finis 2.00 am.

Apr 4
Lovely day. Visiting after lunch. Nice time. Cafe at night.

Apr 5
Lovely and warm. Went to Houdberg for a bath in afternoon. In Jolinet at night. Dancing. Civilians fighting in dumps. Marage afterwards.

Apr 6
Went to Dance at 49 Grand Rue and did not play for a change and had a very nice time.

Apr 7
Lovely day. Usual day. Went a walk in afternoon.

Apr 8
Lovely day. Usual day.

Apr 9
Raining at night. Playing for dance again at 49 Grand Rue. Finished 2.15 am. Home 3.00am

Apr 10
Decent day. Went a walk. Very nice.

Apr 11
Lovely day. Writing in morning. Usual at night.

Apr 12
Usual.

Apr 13
Rotten day. Usual. Playing piano at Rue Leopold.

Apr 14
Changeable. Nice time at night.

Apr 15
Went round to say the many "Goodbyes". Leaving Marage for home at 7.30 pm. Heaps of people to see us off.

Apr 16
Raining. Passed through Valenciennes, Armentierres, Hazebrooke, then to Dunkirk.

Apr 17
At Dunkirk, after a tiring and rotten journey. Went to camp for bath etc and inspection "Short Arm". Then to another camp to sleep under canvas. Cinema at night.

Apr 18
In Dunkirk in morning. Dirty town. Went down "Skin Alley".
What sights of girls. Went to cinema and dancing (all men) at night.
Wagons all loaded.

Apr 19
Leaving Dunkirk at 2.20 pm for Tilbury Docks. Lovely crossing. Calm. Off Dover at 6.00 pm. Anchored off Southend, up Thames for the night.

Apr 20
Went up Thames in morning to Tilbury Docks at 1.00 pm. Had walk in town. Left Tilbury after unloading and loading wagons etc for Gailes Camp. Scotland at 8.00 pm.

Apr 21
Lovely day. What a shame. Passed Leeds, Skipton etc to Carlisle. Dancing on platform for joy. Stopped at Dumfries also.

Apr 22
At Gailes.

Apr 23
At Gailes.

Apr 24
At Gailes. Dance at YM. Fine. Finished 1.00 am.

Apr 25
Left Gailes 11.00 am for Georgetown for Demobb. Went round Glasgow. Left Glasgow at 9.5 pm for Leeds.

Apr 26
At Leeds at 3.10 am. Stayed a while then arrived Bradford 9.30 am. BRADFORD at last. What luck to come back after all the dangers. Went to W in afternoon. W alone. Went to Regent at night.

Apr 27
Snowing. Stayed in bed until 11.00 am. W's after dinner. Stayed in all day. Heavy blizzard at night.

Apr 28
Snow still. Up at 9.00 am. Saw Sharman's. Good day.

Apr 29
Went to Alhambra at night. Grock and partner.

Apr 30
With W. Stayed in town to tea.

MAY

May 1
With W at night. Collisons in afternoon.

May 2
Went with Brad at night.

May 3
Motoring to Hebden. Lovely. Walked with W to Burnsall and Linton.

May 4
Up at W all day.

May 5
Commencing work at Sharman's again. Went to Alhambra with W.

May 6
Getting back to the usual routine of things.

May 23
Month up got my suit etc.

JUNE
June
11
Commenced wool sorting at Illingworth, Wood & Rambothams.

Jun 28
Peace signed at Versailles at 3.00 pm. Not much rejoicing here.

JULY
July 19
Peace celebration day in Bradford. No pageant.

AUGUST
Aug 17
Up at 6.00 am. Off motoring to Scotland at 10.00 am.

1927
Sunday July 24
Opening of Menin Gate by General Plumber in memory of about 59,000 officers and men who fell in salient and have no known grave.

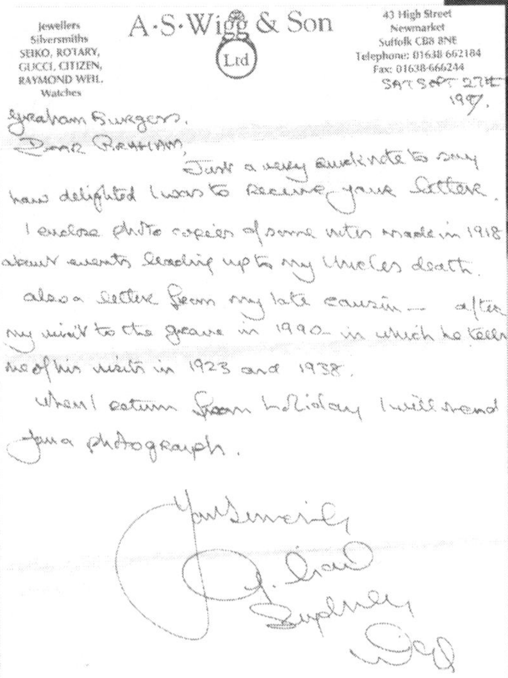

Jewellers
Silversmiths
SEIKO, ROTARY,
GUCCI, CITIZEN,
RAYMOND WEIL
Watches

A·S·Wigg & Son
Ltd

43 High Street
Newmarket
Suffolk CB8 8NE
Telephone: 01638 662184
Fax: 01638 666244

SAT SEPT 27TH
1997.

Graham Burgess.

Dear GRAHAM,

Just a very quick note to say how delighted I was to receive your letter.

I enclose photo copies of some notes made in 1918 about events leading up to my Uncles death.

also a letter from my late cousin — after my visit to the grave in 1990 in which he tells me of his visits in 1923 and 1938.

When I return from holiday I will send you a photograph.

Yours sincerely
A. Sydney Wigg

POSTSCRIPT

In 1996 I took my parents to France and Belgium to visit some of the WWI cemeteries and places which my grandfather had mentioned in his War Record. Amongst the places we visited was a small cemetery near Cambrai where we found the grave of Capt. Wigg for whom my grandfather had been a servant. My mother tells me that her father had often spoken of Capt. Wigg and it seems that they had got along well during the short time they spent together.

As we left, I wondered whether anyone had ever visited this grave before. The visitors' book only recorded relatively recent visits so was not of much help. Once back home I wrote to the War Graves Commission to see whether they had any earlier records or other useful information. They replied that the only information they had was that Capt. Wigg had been from Newmarket.

This was a time before the internet had been fully established, so I went to the library and found altogether eight entries for 'Wigg' in the Newmarket telephone directory. I wrote to each of these asking simply whether they had known of a relative of theirs who had been a captain in the First World War and had been killed just before it ended. Not long afterwards I received a phone call from a Mr Sydney Wigg. We had a long conversation during which he told me that Capt. Wigg had been his uncle and that he had been named after him. This Mr Wigg had, indeed, visited the grave and had taken a keen interest in the war. His family had been told at the time that Capt. Wigg had been killed by a stun grenade; my grandfather's War Record tells a rather different story.

I sent a photocopy of the handwritten War Record to Mr. Wigg, and he sent me a photograph of his uncle, Captain Sydney Wigg, who was killed on 13th October 1918, aged 29. It felt curiously satisfying to have made these links on behalf of our long-departed relatives.

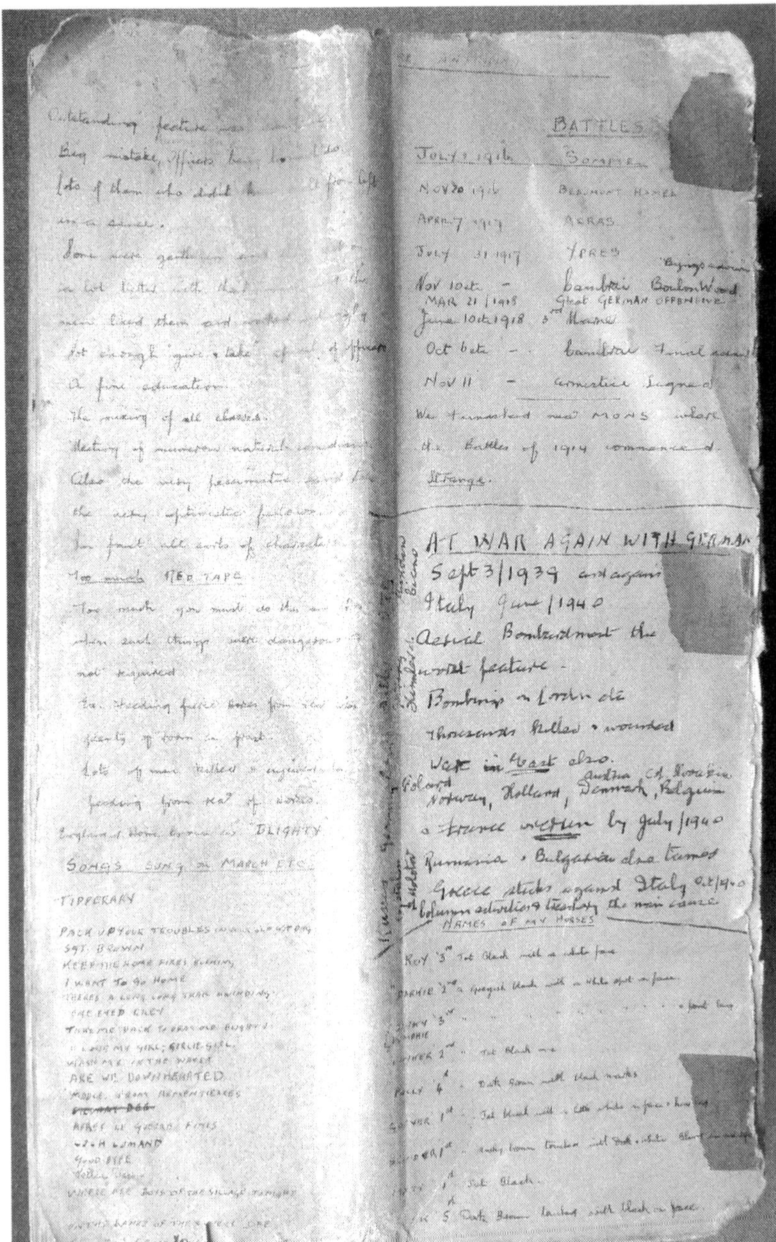

Outstanding feature was ...
Big mistake, officers being ...
lots of them who didn't ... for life
in a sense.
Some were gentlemen and ...
in lot better with the ... the
men liked them and worked ...
Not enough "give & take" spirit of officers
A fine education.
The mixing of all classes.
Meeting of numerous natural conditions
Also the very pessimistic ...
the very optimistic fellows.
In fact all sorts of characters
Too much RED TAPE
Too much you must do this ...
when such things were dangerous ...
not required
Ex. stealing ... horses from ...
plenty of ... in front.
Lots of men killed & injured ...
... from ... of horses.
England & home known as "BLIGHTY"

SONGS SUNG ON MARCH ETC.

TIPPERARY
PACK UP YOUR TROUBLES IN YOUR OLD KIT BAG
SGT. BROWN
KEEP THE HOME FIRES BURNING
I WANT TO GO HOME
THERE'S A LONG LONG TRAIL AWINDING
SHE EYED GREY
TAKE ME BACK TO DEAR OLD BLIGHTY
I LOVE MY GIRL; GIRLIE GIRL
WASH ME IN THE WATER
ARE WE DOWNHEARTED
MADEMOISELLE FROM ARMENTIERES
~~[illegible]~~
... FIRES
... LAND
GOOD BYEE
...
WHERE ARE THE BOYS OF THE VILLAGE TONIGHT
ON THE BANKS OF THE ...

BATTLES

July 1 1916	Somme
Nov 20 1916	Beaumont Hamel
April 7 1917	Arras
July 31 1917	Ypres
Nov 10th –	Cambrai Bourlon Wood
Mar 21 / 1918	Great GERMAN OFFENSIVE
June 10th 1918	2nd Marne
Oct 6th –	Cambrai Final assault
Nov 11 –	Armistice Signed

We ... near MONS where the Battles of 1914 commenced.
Strange.

AT WAR AGAIN WITH GERMANY
Sept 3/1939 and again
Italy June/1940
Aerial Bombardment the worst feature –
Bombings in London etc
thousands killed & wounded
... in West also.
Poland, Norway, Holland, Austria, Cz. Slovakia, Denmark, Belgium
& France ... by July/1940
Rumania & Bulgaria also ...
Greece sticks against Italy Oct/1940
... the main cause

NAMES OF MY HORSES

ROY 3rd Jet Black with a white face
... 2nd a greyish black with a white spot on face
...
... 1st Jet Black
... 5 Dark Brown ... black on face

APPENDIX

Back cover text

Remarks re-anything
Outstanding feature was discipline.
Big mistake, officers being too much so.
Lots of them who didn't know right from left in a sense.
Some were gentlemen and they got on a lot better with their men, and the men liked them and worked willingly. Not enough "give and take" spirit of officers.
A fine education.
The mixing of all classes.
Meeting of numerous natural comedians. Also the very pessimistic to the very optimistic fellows. In fact all sorts of characters.
Too much RED TAPE.
Too much you must do this and that when such things were dangerous and not required.
Feeding fierce horses from rear when plenty of room in front. Lots of men killed and injured feeding from rear of horses.
England or home known as 'Blighty'

Songs sung on march etc.
Tipperary
Pack up your troubles in your old kit bag
Sgt. Brown
Keep the home fires burning
I want to go home
There's a long long trail a winding
One eyed Riley
Take me back to dear old Blighty
I love my girl, girly girl

Wash me in the water
Are we downhearted
Moole[?] from Armentierres
Apres le guerre finis
Loch Lomond
Good -byee
Nellie Dean
Where are the boys of the village tonight
On the banks of the silvery Dee
Far, far from Ypres I want to be

Battles
July 1916 Somme
Nov 20 1916 Beaumont Hamel
April 7 1917 Arras
July 31 1917 Ypres
Nov 10 etc – Cambrai, Bourlon Wood
March 1918 Great German offensive
June 10th etc. 1918 Marne
Oct 6 etc. Cambrai, final assault
Nov 11 Armistice signed

We finished at Mons where the battles of 1914 commenced. Strange.

Names of my horses
Roy 3rd Jet black with a white face
Darkie 2nd A greyish black with a white spot on face
Dinky/Dumphie 3rd A greyish black with a white spot on front leg
Tinker 2nd Jet black one
Polly 4th Dark brown with black marks
Goayer 1st Jet black with little white on face and hind leg
Blinder 1st Musky brown touched with dark and white.
Blind in one eye.
Mary 4th Jet black
Jock 5th Dark brown touched with black on face.

At war again with Germany

Sept 3rd 1939 and again Italy June 1940

Aerial bombardment the worst feature. Bombing of London etc. Thousands killed and wounded.

War in East also.Poland, Norway, Holland, Austria, Czechoslovakia, Denmark, Belgium and France overrun by July 1940. Rumania and Bulgaria also turned. Greece sticks against Italy Oct 1940. 5th Column activities and treachery the main cause.

Russia, Stalin, Molotov

Germany Brutes

Hitler

Goerring

Himmler etc.

Italy

Mussolini

Bicno[?]

Harry on holiday with his wife Winifred and their daughter Jean, my mother, in the early 1930s.

35683986R00081

Made in the USA
Charleston, SC
16 November 2014